CONTENTS

JUDGE
FOR YOURSELF

INTRODUCTION

Indian leader Mohandas Karamchand Gandhi was among the greatest social and political reformers of recent times. In the early 20th century, he struggled to achieve racial justice in South Africa. However he is best remembered for his later campaigns to overthrow British rule in India, which finally led to the country's declaration of independence in 1947. Gandhi's career was marked by dedication to non-violence, compassion and tolerance, virtues inspired by his Hindu faith. His selflessness earned him the honorary title Mahatma, a Hindi word meaning 'great soul'.

This book looks at Gandhi and his activities in two different ways. In the first part, you can read the straightforward story of his life, from his birth in 1869 to his assassination in 1948. This part is divided into chapters in the normal way, and also includes feature spreads that highlight two special subjects, the Raj and religion in India.

In the second part of the book, you can examine the main themes of Gandhi's life, for example his beliefs and campaigns, more closely. To help you assess Gandhi's ideals and actions for yourself, this part is divided into sections, each headed with an important question to consider. The first two pages below each question provide one possible answer, together with quotations, statistics and other facts to back it up. The next two pages provide a second potential answer, also with supporting evidence and information.

The question pages can be used in several ways. You may simply want to read them through, look at both possible answers and sets of sources for each question, then make up your own mind. You could also write down the reasons for your decision.

INDIA, PAKISTAN AND BANGLADESH

Before 1947, India covered a larger area than it does today. However, when the country gained its independence, it was partitioned into two separate nations: India and Pakistan (see page 39). Pakistan was itself divided into the territories of East and West Pakistan, which were both in the north and separated by land that remained Indian. In 1971, civil war broke out between East and West, and finally East Pakistan declared its independence as the new state of Bangladesh. For most of Gandhi's life, however, his country was in its original, undivided form. So unless stated otherwise, that is what the term 'India' refers to in this book.

Before dedicating his life to the struggle for Indian independence, Gandhi was a lawyer and often dressed in European-style clothing.

Britain officially granted India independence on 15 August 1947. Here, young Indians in Calcutta celebrate the occasion.

During his later years, Gandhi lived very simply. He ate sparingly, wore traditional garments and spent time praying and spinning cloth.

Alternatively, the material could be used for a classroom debate between two groups, each arguing for a different answer. The pages may also serve as a prompt to further research. For example, you may wish to find more data to back a particular view of Gandhi's *satyagraha* ideals or treatment of the untouchables.

The question pages have another purpose, too. They are designed to show you that facts and statistics can be used to support completely different points of view. That is why historians have to sift through a great deal of material, from a wide variety of sources, before they can reach reliable conclusions about the past. Even then, answers are rarely clear-cut and may be overturned by new evidence. So, as you consider the questions, remember that neither of the answers provided may be completely correct. Using all the information in both parts of the book, and any more that you can find, it is up to you to judge for yourself.

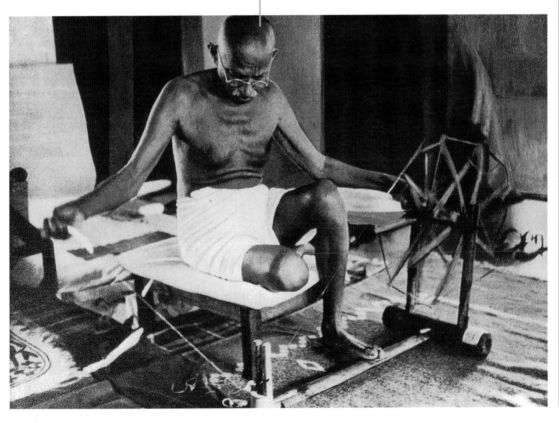

THE EARLY YEARS

The bustling Indian city of Porbandar, in the north-western state of Gujarat, stands on the coast of the Arabian Sea. Mohandas Karamchand Gandhi was born on 2 October 1869 in one of the many large, white-stone houses that line the narrow streets of the port.

FAMILY BACKGROUND

Gandhi's family was of some importance in Porbandar. His father, called Karamchand but often known as Kaba, was the city's prime minister, as his father had been. In this role, he was answerable to the local prince, who was not officially under British rule (see pages 20–21). However, the British government in Delhi kept a watchful eye on all the principalities of the region and had ultimate power over them.

A statue of Gandhi now stands in Porbandar, the city where he was born and grew up.

Karamchand had already had three wives before he married a much younger woman called Putlibai. She gave birth to her fourth and final child, Gandhi himself, when she was just 25 years old but her husband was 47. In total, Karamchand had six children: three daughters and three sons.

RELIGION AND CASTE

The Gandhis were followers of the Hindu religion (see pages 28–29). As members of the Vaisya (merchant) caste and Banias (grocer) sub-caste, they were not of high rank. Nevertheless, they were devout and gave special allegiance to the god Vishnu. Gandhi's mother also prayed and fasted regularly. She made sure that her family ate a vegetarian diet, following Hindu beliefs.

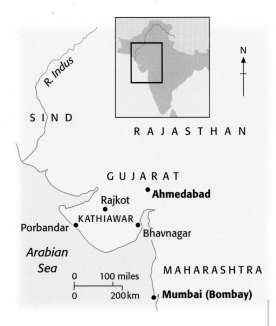

This map shows the corner of north-west India where Gandhi spent his early years. The main places mentioned in this chapter are marked.

Jain holy men cover their mouths with a muslin mask or piece of cloth so that they do not breathe in, and so kill, any flying insects.

Her Hinduism was, however, unusual in one respect. She belonged to a group called the Pranamis, which incorporated some Islamic beliefs into its philosophy.

When reminiscing later in life, Gandhi recalled that he had been his mother's 'pet child', and that her saintliness, unwavering religious observance and willingness to find truth in religions other than her own had made a great impression on him. As a young boy, he was also influenced by Jainism, an ancient Indian religion which flourished in and around Porbandar. Jains preach an extreme form of *ahimsa* (non-violence), a belief that outlaws the harming of any creature. During his future political campaigns, Gandhi was always to practise non-violence.

SCHOOL DAYS

When Gandhi was about seven, his father was appointed to a different post. He now

Gandhi in Porbandar, aged seven. At about this time he began to attend school, an experience that he did not much enjoy.

became the Prime Minister of Rajkot, a city about 200 kilometres inland from Porbandar, with another ruler. The young Mohandas started school in this new environment. He was not an outstanding pupil and had little genuine interest in his studies. Nor was he particularly happy. Although playful among his family, he was shy at school and ran home at the day's end to avoid speaking to classmates.

Despite his indifference to education, Gandhi learned important moral lessons in these early years. For example, he discovered that he could not bring himself to cheat in a spelling test, even when his teacher urged him to do so to impress an inspector. He was also guided by religious tales that he learned outside school hours. His favourite was a play about a king called Harishchandra, who obeyed the gods' demands to sacrifice his wealth and status. In his autobiography, Gandhi later wrote: 'To follow truth and to go through all the ordeals Harishchandra went through was the one ideal it [the play] inspired in me.'

Gandhi's father, Karamchand. Gandhi once described him as 'truthful, brave and generous, but short-tempered'.

AN EARLY MARRIAGE

Gandhi moved on to a high school, where his two brothers were already pupils. There he began to show more academic promise. However when he was 13, his studies were interrupted by a major event in his personal life that was to bring him both great happiness and great sorrow.

Among Hindu families it was common practice for parents to choose acceptable spouses for their children without consulting them. By his teens, Gandhi had already been betrothed three times. The first two girls selected to become his wife had died one after the other. But the third, a girl called Kasturbai from Porbandar, had survived to reach marriageable age. When Gandhi's father began to arrange a joint wedding for one of his older sons and a nephew, he realized that he could save money by making it a triple celebration. So Mohandas and Kasturbai, both little more than children, were included in his plans.

The wedding took place in Porbandar in 1882. There was high drama at the outset. Gandhi's father had not been permitted to leave his place of employment in Rajkot until the last moment. Then he had had to travel at breakneck speed by stagecoach in order to arrive in time for the festivities. The coach, however, had fallen over during the journey, seriously injuring its passenger. As a result, Gandhi's father arrived bandaged and in pain. Nevertheless, the ceremony went ahead.

Gandhi took a childish pleasure in the proceedings and earnestly took his vows. Married life back in Rajkot, however, proved more difficult. Kasturbai was uneducated, but had a strong will and a sharp tongue that cut through the young Gandhi's sometimes rather pompous pronouncements. She also stubbornly resisted his efforts to teach her to read and write. Gandhi, for his part, became a jealous husband. The couple were sexually active from the beginning of their life together and, fearful of rivals, he attempted to confine his wife to their home.

Teenage temptations

After missing almost a year of school because of his marriage, Gandhi returned to his studies. Now he began to win prizes for his classwork, but did his best to avoid sports, in which he took no pleasure.

During these early teenage years, Gandhi also gave in to several temptations forbidden to Hindus. In particular, he was persuaded by a friend called Mehtab that the British were able to rule India because meat-eating made them strong. So, for about a year, Gandhi periodically ate goat and other meat. Eventually, however, his sense of guilt, coupled with the stress of keeping this secret from his parents, made him return to strict vegetarianism. A similar experiment with smoking, which also involved stealing money to pay for cigarettes, did not last much longer.

An incident that caused both Gandhi and his family even greater distress occurred a little later, when he was 15. It began when he removed some of the gold from an armlet belonging to his brother, in order to pay off that same brother's debts. Even though he had not committed the theft for personal gain, Gandhi was once more unable to live with the guilt. So he confessed to his father, who by then was confined to bed through illness. His father's forgiveness, which was offered without reproach, was a moral lesson that Gandhi never forgot.

A death in the family

By the time Gandhi was 16, his father was extremely ill. So, as well as devoting time to his studies and his newly pregnant wife, the teenager shared with his mother and a servant the demanding task of nursing him. While Gandhi took care of his father's physical needs, some of Karamchand's many friends – Muslims, Jains and Parsis, as well as

Hindus – came to offer him spiritual comfort. Through listening to them, Gandhi found that his own religious understanding increased.

Despite everyone's efforts, it soon became clear Gandhi's father would not recover – neither Ayurvedic nor other medicines improved his condition, and the family rejected the possibility of surgery. The end came one evening, just after Gandhi had accepted an uncle's offer to take his place at the sick man's bedside. Minutes later, when he was back in his own bedroom with his young wife, a servant rushed in to tell him Karamchand had died. Gandhi never forgave himself for leaving his father at that crucial moment. Some weeks after, his misery deepened when his first child died after clinging to life for just a few days.

New beginnings

Haunted by his father's death though he was, Gandhi was now able to devote more time to his studies. In 1887, he passed his matriculation examination, which marked the end of

Ahmedabad, where Gandhi sat his matriculation examination. In 1915, he founded an ashram near the city centre.

his high school years. Then, encouraged by his family, he enrolled at Samaldas College in the city of Bhavnagar, to the south-east of Rajkot. By his own admission, however, Gandhi could not understand the lectures and soon found himself 'entirely at sea'. As a result, he left the college after just one term.

Gandhi's relatives now had to decide what he should do next. His father had always wanted one of his sons to follow in his own prime ministerial footsteps. A learned family friend, Mavji Dave, advised that the best way for Gandhi to achieve this ambition was to go to London and there study to be a barrister. In Dave's view, a qualification from England would guarantee Gandhi a good political post on his return.

Gandhi happily agreed to this plan, even though it meant leaving behind his wife and baby son Harilal, who was born in 1888.

Putlibai, however, was reluctant to see her youngest son depart overseas. She also feared the meat-eating, alcohol-drinking, tobacco-smoking and other temptations that awaited him far away in London. Still, after a Jain monk persuaded Gandhi to take a vow in which he promised to abstain from wine, women and meat, she finally gave her blessing to the trip.

Leaving for London

This obstacle overcome, Gandhi made his way to the great port city of Mumbai (Bombay), from where he planned to set sail. But then another problem arose. A meeting of the Bania caste elders was called, where

In 1888, Gandhi set sail for England from the coastal city of Mumbai. The Gateway of India arch shown here was not built until 1927.

Gandhi was told that no Bania had ever been to England, and that such a visit was against the principles of his religion. What is more, if he went, he would be expelled from the caste and forbidden even to associate with its members. Despite these threats, Gandhi refused to change his mind.

The 18-year-old Gandhi eventually sailed out of Mumbai on 4 September 1888. At this time, he spoke English only falteringly – his native language was Gujarati. Nevertheless, he was determined to play the part of the English gentleman and accordingly bought formal suits and ties to replace his traditional Indian clothing.

In 1890, Gandhi visited Paris from his base in England. He went up the newly built Eiffel Tower, but later dismissed it as a 'trinket'.

ENGLISH EXPERIENCES

When Gandhi's ship was approaching the English port of Southampton, he prepared himself by dressing in a white flannel suit. Then, unaware that this was not suitable clothing for a foggy autumn day, he disembarked and made his way to London's Victoria Hotel. Soon after, he found more congenial lodgings with a succession of English families. However, homesickness and the scarcity of vegetarian food – vegetarianism was then rare in England – made the early weeks of his visit a trial.

Gandhi now resolved to make greater efforts to fit in to English society. So he bought himself new, London-made suits, as well as a top hat. He also took elocution, dancing, violin and French lessons that he could ill afford. However, he soon came to his senses and dedicated himself instead to the legal studies that were the real reason for his stay. In addition, he decided to take another examination, the London Matriculation, which involved studying Latin and several other subjects.

Gandhi also expanded his mind in other ways. Encouraged by English books in defence of vegetarianism, he now wholeheartedly embraced its ideals. Through mixing with Theosophists, he discovered more about the Indian religions of Hinduism and Buddhism (see pages 28–29) and was persuaded to read the *Bhagavad Gita*, finding it 'of priceless worth'. Despite his reservations about Christianity – Christian missionaries in India had mocked Hinduism – Gandhi read the Bible, too. The Sermon on the Mount in particular impressed him greatly.

THE RETURN TO INDIA

Gandhi worked hard for his legal examinations, far harder than he needed in fact, since people rarely failed. After passing, he was called to the Bar (made a barrister) on 10 June 1891. Just two days later, some two years and eight months after he had arrived in England, he began the long return journey to the land of his birth.

CHAPTER TWO

SOUTH AFRICA

Shortly after the 22-year-old Gandhi sailed back into Mumbai, he learned that his much-loved mother had died. In his autobiography, he relates that this news came as a 'severe shock', but that nevertheless he 'took to life just as though nothing had happened.' Soon, however, he was facing other problems that demanded a much more active response.

CASTE CONFLICT

Gandhi had gone to England with the blessing of his family, but against the wishes of his sub-caste (see pages 10–11). So on his return home, he decided to attempt a reconciliation. He was successful only in part. The Rajkot section of the caste readmitted him, but the Porbandar section, to which Kasturbai's family belonged, refused to welcome him back.

Gandhi's family life came under pressure for other reasons, too. Jealousy continued to make him suspicious of Kasturbai's every move. He also raged against her unwillingness to learn reading and writing, and to accept the customs that he introduced into their Rajkot household. These included the requirement to eat with a knife and fork, rather than with the hand in the Indian manner, and to wear European-style clothes.

LEGAL LIFE

Gandhi's most pressing problem in 1891, however, was his need to earn a living. His family's reputation had diminished greatly since the death of his father, so it seemed unlikely any local prince would give him a political job. He therefore had no option but to try his hand as a lawyer, and with that intention set out for Mumbai. His new career soon ended in disaster. For his first case, Gandhi worked himself up into a frenzy of apprehension. As a result, when he rose to cross-examine witnesses, he found himself unable to speak and had to leave the court.

A FRIEND IN NEED?

After this fiasco, Gandhi returned to Rajkot, where he prepared legal documents for poor people who had to attend court. But soon he was involved in another upset. His elder brother had once worked for a member of the local princely family. This man had since become prince, and now accused the brother of having given him bad advice. The case was to be heard by Porbandar's British administrator, Charles Ollivant.

As luck would have it, Gandhi had made Ollivant's acquaintance in England, so agreed to speak to him on his brother's behalf. To his astonishment, he was insulted and thrown out of the administrator's office. Now Gandhi began to recognize that the British did not always wield their power justly in India. No longer willing to work in courts under Ollivant's control, he began urgently looking for a job elsewhere.

SOUTH AFRICA

The perfect opportunity presented itself soon afterwards, when Gandhi's brother received a letter from Dada Abdulla and Co. This Porbandar-based firm of Muslim merchants was involved in a case against another Gujarati firm in South Africa, and was looking for a legally trained, English-speaking Gujarati to assist its lawyers. Gandhi took up the offer, and in April 1893 began the voyage to Durban. He left behind his wife and two children – a second son, Manilal, had been born in 1892.

In the late 19th century, South Africa was a divided land controlled by some 750,000 European settlers. The territories of Cape Colony and Natal were under British colonial rule, while Dutch people known as Boers (farmers) dominated the territories of the Transvaal and Orange Free State. The original black inhabitants, of whom there were more than two million, had struggled without success to remain free.

With about 100,000 members, South Africa's Indian population was also substantial. Many of these people had come to the country as indentured labourers, and worked for pitiful wages down mines and on sugar plantations. Europeans regarded them all as inferior and called them 'coolies' or 'samis'. Muslims and Parsis were, however, given some respect, while Hindus were considered the lowest of the low.

JOURNEY TO PRETORIA

After spending a week in Durban, Gandhi took the train to Pretoria, the Transvaal city where he was to work. As was his custom, he travelled first class. That evening when the train stopped at Maritzburg, a white passenger entered Gandhi's carriage. Then he quickly fetched the train guards, demanding they remove this 'coloured' man from the first-class section. Outraged, Gandhi refused to budge, so was thrown off.

During the freezing night he then spent in a waiting room, Gandhi asked himself whether to give up and return to India, or to stay and fight against prejudice. His sense of duty left him little option. So the following evening, he boarded another train to continue his trip. Its next stop was Charlestown, where passengers disembarked, then continued by stagecoach before picking up the train again in Johannesburg.

Now Gandhi experienced the reality of racial discrimination once more. First, the man

This map shows South Africa as it was when Gandhi lived there. All the main places mentioned in this chapter are marked.

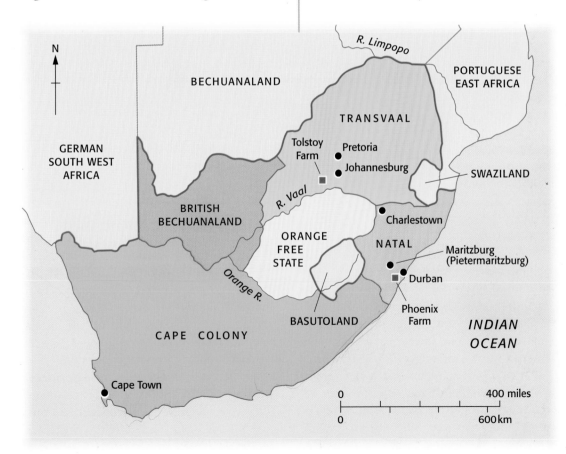

in charge of the stagecoach forced him to sit on top rather than inside. Then he tried to make him move to the footboard, under the driver's feet. When Gandhi protested, the man beat him up. Gandhi's misfortunes continued in Johannesburg, where he was denied a hotel room simply on account of his race. But despite all these unhappy encounters, he finally reached Pretoria in a first-class train carriage.

FIGHTING PREJUDICE

Gandhi soon found lodgings and began his legal work. At the same time, he set out to combat the anti-Indian prejudice that was particularly strong in the Transvaal and Orange Free State. In neither territory, for example, were Indians allowed to vote. In the Transvaal, they were not permitted even to walk on public footpaths, or to go out after nine in the evening without a pass. The threat of deportation was also constant.

Gandhi decided the best way to start his campaign was to call a meeting of all Pretoria's Indians. When he addressed the group, he found he was not tongue-tied as he had been in the Mumbai court. On the contrary, he spoke with great fervour about the need for Indians to be truthful in their business dealings. He also suggested that they should stop worrying about the differences between Hindus, Muslims and others, and instead join together in an association to defend their rights.

The Indians took Gandhi's advice and began to hold regular meetings. He did all he could to support them, while at the same time developing his religious ideas. Attempts by South African friends to convert him to Christianity led Gandhi to read many Christian books, including *The Kingdom of God Is Within You* by famous Russian novelist Leo Tolstoy (see page 42). However, he was not convinced by the central beliefs of the faith, so also took the time to explore Hinduism and Islam.

Gandhi surrounded by his staff at the offices of his law firm in Johannesburg (see page 17). There is no hint in this conventional picture that he would ever be anything but a rich professional man.

A TURNING POINT

Dada Abdulla and Co won its case early in 1894. As he therefore no longer had any work to do, Gandhi travelled south to Durban with the intention of boarding a steamship back to Mumbai. To bid him farewell, the Indian community arranged a dinner in his honour. While Gandhi was sitting at the table, he noticed a newspaper article headed 'Indian Franchise'. It dealt with a new bill that, if passed, would remove Indians' right to vote for members of the Natal legislature.

Gandhi quickly drew the attention of his fellow diners to the article and encouraged them to protest against this development. They were willing, but asked Gandhi to postpone his departure for a month to help them. He readily agreed and so began his political career. Or, to use his own words, 'Thus God laid the foundations of my life in South Africa and sowed the seed of the fight for national self-respect.'

During the next few weeks, Gandhi founded the Natal Indian Congress, an organization inspired by the Indian National Congress (see box), arranged petitions against the Franchise Bill, and publicized the Indians' fight. Eventually, he became so involved in the struggle that he was persuaded to settle in Natal in order to continue his public work. At the same time, he established a private legal practice as a barrister.

RETURN TO INDIA

By 1896, Gandhi had won two victories. The Franchise Bill had been redrafted so that some Indians were able to vote, and a proposed £25 annual tax on indentured labourers had been reduced to £3. Now the young lawyer decided the time had come to bring his family to South Africa, so went back to

India to fetch them. During his return home, he wrote *The Green Pamphlet*, a publication that explained the grievances of the 'coolies'. He also made several public speeches on the subject. Then he, Kasturbai and their sons journeyed westwards once more.

When Gandhi's ship reached Durban, it was not allowed to dock for over three weeks. This was because news about his pamphlet and speeches, much of it inaccurate, had reached South Africa and angered the white inhabitants. As a result, they were not prepared to welcome Gandhi back. When he did finally make his way off, he was beaten up.

THE BOER WAR

Despite the hostility he met on his return, Gandhi continued his work for the Natal Indian Congress. At the same time, he built up his legal practice

A French magazine cover from 1899 showing a confrontation between Boers and British in the city of Mafeking.

THE INDIAN NATIONAL CONGRESS

The British effectively ruled India from the mid-19th century (see pages 20–21). Many Indians, however, believed that they, the native people of the sub-continent, should have a greater influence on policy-making. So, too, did some British administrators, including Allan Hume, a Scot. It was largely as a result of his support that the Indian National Congress was established in 1885 with the purpose of achieving this aim.

When Gandhi returned to India in 1896 and 1901, he met the leaders of the two main camps into which the Congress was already dividing. Bal Gangadhar Tilak, an extremist Hindu Brahman (see pages

28–29), led the nationalist faction. It wanted to expel the British and establish home rule. Gopal Krishna Gokhale, another Brahman, believed there was no real alternative to British rule, but hoped to give Indians more power by changing the constitution. In 1906 a third group, Congress's Muslim minority, broke away to form the Muslim League.

Until Gandhi took charge in the 1920s (see page 16), the Indian National Congress did little more than endlessly discuss the possibility of change. However, under his guidance, it became a leading force in the campaigns designed to drive the British out of India (see page 27 onwards).

The Indian Ambulance Corps. Gandhi himself is seated in the centre of the middle row, with another man's hand resting on his shoulder.

so that it provided a substantial income. Nor was family life forgotten – in 1897, Gandhi became the father of a third son, Ramdas.

Although Gandhi abhorred the mistreatment of Indians in Natal, he did not blame this state of affairs on the British Empire. On the contrary, he was unswervingly loyal to this vast agglomeration of territories under the control of the government in London. The Empire, in his view, was not responsible for difficulties in individual colonies – the fault lay in local problems. For this reason, when war broke out between British and Boers over control of the Transvaal in 1899 (a first Boer War had ended in British defeat in 1881), he supported Britain.

In fact, Gandhi did more than offer his support – he set up and served in the Indian Ambulance Corps, an organization of some 1,100 members. The war ended in victory for Britain in 1902, when the Transvaal and the Orange Free State became British colonies.

NEW CHALLENGES

Gandhi's ambulance work did not continue throughout the war. In 1901 his whole family, including Devadas, a fourth son born the previous year, returned to India. There Gandhi set up a legal practice in Mumbai and also began to interest himself in the Indian National Congress (see page 15), some of whose members were already agitating for independence from Britain. But then, in early 1902, he received a telegram from Durban.

Before leaving South Africa, Gandhi had promised to return if his Indian friends there needed him. It now seemed that they did, and urgently. Not only was their situation steadily worsening, but the Colonial Secretary, Joseph Chamberlain, was about to pay a visit. The Indians wanted to prepare a document that would explain their complaints to him, but did not feel able to do so without Gandhi's help.

Gandhi hurried back, leaving his family behind in India. But despite his best efforts, Chamberlain took little notice of his carefully worded statement. Now the main aim of the government in London was to rebuild relations with the Boers. The sufferings of

Indians, or indeed of the native black population, were of little interest. Gandhi realized he would have to return full-time to the fray if progress were to be made. So he set up a new legal business in Johannesburg in the Transvaal.

PHOENIX FARM

Gandhi now used all his skills to work for the Transvaal Indians. In particular, he argued strongly against the discriminatory regulations that began to pour out of the colony's new Asiatic Department. In 1904, he also set up *Indian Opinion*, a newspaper for the Indian community.

A more important development soon followed. As Gandhi was starting a train journey one night, a friend thrust a book into his hand. It was *Unto This Last*, by English art and social critic John Ruskin (see page 42). The book spoke of the virtues of the simple life, of the equal worth of every individual, and of the value of physical labour. By dawn, Gandhi had made up his mind to put these principles into practice.

The result of Gandhi's decision was the establishment of Phoenix Farm, also known as Phoenix Settlement, on some 40 hectares of land near Durban in 1904. Its inhabitants tilled the soil, produced *Indian Opinion*, and tried to live in tune with Gandhi's principles of simplicity and hard work. Gandhi himself sometimes stayed there, too, but he also kept his house in Johannesburg, where his wife and young family soon joined him again.

A LIFE-CHANGING DECISION

In 1906, Natal's Zulus rebelled against their British rulers. Wishing to be of assistance, Gandhi reformed the Indian Ambulance Corps and left his Johannesburg home for good. While his family settled at Phoenix Farm, he and his fellow corps members spent their time caring for wounded Zulus, whom white medical staff would not touch. Gandhi came to believe that the 'rebellion' was in fact a 'man-hunt' directed against the Zulus. His

Gandhi's wife, Kasturbai, and their four sons in 1902. The youngest, Devadas, was about two at this time.

Bambaata (front left) was the leader of the 1906 Zulu 'rebellion'. Here, he is surrounded by some of his warriors.

already dwindling faith in the British was reduced even further as a result.

The Ambulance Corps often had to march for hours. Gandhi used this time to think and came to a life-changing decision. Now he concluded that it was right to end his sexual relationship with his wife, in order to commit himself fully to the wider community and to spiritual matters. So, in mid-1906, he took the vow of *brahmacharya* (celibacy and self-restraint). Fortunately, his wife did not mind.

THE BLACK LAW

While still in the corps, Gandhi heard that the Transvaal government had proposed a new 'Black Law'. If passed, it would require all Indians to register with the authorities, to carry their registration certificates, and to have their fingerprints taken. The law would also give the police power to enter Indian homes in order to check documents. Muslims particularly objected to this idea, as Muslim women lived in *purdah*.

Outrage at the proposed law soon grew, and on 11 September 1906, a mass meeting to discuss opposition tactics was held at the Empire Theatre in Johannesburg. At Gandhi's urging, the participants took an oath saying they would resist registration whatever the personal cost. In the event, the British government refused to sanction the law. However on 1 January 1907, the Transvaal became self-governing again and the Asiatic Registration Act was quickly passed. It differed from the proposed Black Act only in excluding women from its provisions.

SATYAGRAHA

Gandhi now decided to try to stop the law coming into effect. His plan was to use non-violent tactics that came to be known collectively as *satyagraha* (see page 46). This Hindi word is often translated as 'passive resistance', but really means 'truth force'. Its practitioners were not to use physical power to get their way, but to be full of the spiritual power that came from knowing they were acting in accordance with the truth. They were also to be ready to suffer, even die, for their beliefs.

The *satyagrahis* began their campaign by refusing to register. Soon the Transvaal government started arresting these law-breakers, and in January 1908, Gandhi himself was given a two-month prison sentence. After a false dawn, when it appeared the government would repeal the law if Indians agreed to register voluntarily, the campaign began in earnest again. In 1909, Gandhi went to England to seek the British government's support for his cause, but without success.

THE UNION OF SOUTH AFRICA

A new era in South Africa's history started in 1910, when its provinces joined to form the Union of South Africa. Louis Botha became the dominion's prime minister, and General Jan Smuts its minister of the interior. Gandhi, meanwhile, continued his experiments in communal living by setting up a second retreat, Tolstoy Farm in the Transvaal.

In 1912, the tension between the South African authorities and the Indians living under their rule increased dramatically. During that year, Gopal Krishna Gokhale, a leader of the Indian National Congress (see box page 15), visited Smuts in South Africa. In the aftermath, the registration law was effectively repealed. But the £3 indentured labourer tax, which Gokhale believed Smuts had promised to end, remained in place.

General Smuts became Prime Minister of South Africa after Gandhi had left.

Gandhi (seated left) with two of his European supporters shortly before the 1913 miners' march in South Africa.

A GROWING CAMPAIGN

Gandhi now decided to make abolition of the tax another aim of his *satyagraha* movement. In this way, he won the support of thousands of poor labourers. The number of *satyagrahis* increased further in 1913, when a judge in the Cape Colony declared only Christian marriages were valid. This was a terrible slur on the honour of Hindu, Muslim and Parsi women, so many of them now joined Gandhi's campaign, too.

Indians had long been illegally crossing the border between Natal and the Transvaal in order to challenge the rules that restricted their movements. From 1913, this tactic was more widely practised, and the 'invaders' often ended up in jail. One border crossing that year was to have particularly far-reaching results. After some women from Tolstoy Farm had made their way from the Transvaal to Natal, they headed for the coal-mining town of Newcastle. There they urged Indian

miners to strike against the £3 tax. Soon thousands of men had stopped work.

THE MINERS' MARCH

Now Gandhi arrived to take charge. He decided the best move would be to organize a miners' march back across the border into the Transvaal, then on to Tolstoy Farm. So on 28 October 1913, a procession of over 2,000 men, women and children set out. On the way, Gandhi repeatedly contacted General Smuts, now defence minister, to advise him that if the £3 tax were abolished, he would call off the march at once.

The authorities, however, simply imprisoned Gandhi. Then, when the other marchers were approaching Johannesburg, they put them on trains to concentration camps back in Newcastle. This heavy-handedness led to further strikes by miners and plantation workers. It also won further sympathy for the Indians' cause around the world.

HEADING FOR HOME

Embarrassed by the bad publicity, the South African government now agreed to set up a commission to consider the Indian community's demands. Gandhi was not impressed, as not a single member was Indian, so began to prepare a second march. But then, South Africa's white railway workers staged an unrelated strike that plunged the country into turmoil. Gandhi promised that the *satyagrahis* would discontinue their protests until the matter was resolved. In this way, he earned further public support and virtually obliged General Smuts to negotiate.

The result of the negotiations was the 1914 Indian Relief Act. Its many provisions included the recognition of non-Christian marriages, the abolition of the £3 tax and the gradual ending of indentured labour. By this time a shaven-headed, simply dressed 44-year-old, Gandhi now felt free to leave South Africa. After his ship sailed away in July 1914, Smuts wrote: 'The saint has left our shores.'

THE RAJ

In 1526, India was invaded from the north by a Muslim people known as the Mughals. Spreading gradually south, they took control of many Hindu kingdoms, but often governed through existing rulers. During the same period, a strong European presence was also established in India. By the mid-1600s, the Portuguese, British, French, Dutch and Danes all had trading posts there. However, over the next 200 years, Britain ousted all its rivals to establish the Raj, the British government of India against which Gandhi and his followers were later to struggle so hard.

BRITAIN AND FRANCE

The Portuguese were the first Europeans to reach India, in 1498. The first British trading post was set up at Masulipatam on the east coast in 1611. It was run by the East India Company, which soon established more. Rivalry then developed between Britain and France, which was building up its own territories through the French East India Company.

The last great Mughal emperor, Aurangzeb, died in 1707, and Mughal influence started to decline. Other Indian powers, particularly the Hindu Maratha states in the west, now took the opportunity to increase their power. At the same time, Britain and France set out to seize more territory, and in 1744 war broke out between them. In 1757, the British under Robert Clive defeated a combined force of French and Indians at Plassey, thus acquiring Bengal and surrounding lands. Then, in 1761, British victory at Pondicherry ended France's power in India.

TAKING CONTROL

Following these successes, Britain's influence in India increased further. In 1784, the first of a series of India Acts began to bring the East India Company's private lands under the control of the British government. Meanwhile, the Company's forces were defeating many local Indian leaders. An important victory in 1799 ousted Tipu Sultan, Muslim ruler of the

Tipu Sultan's burial place in Mysore.

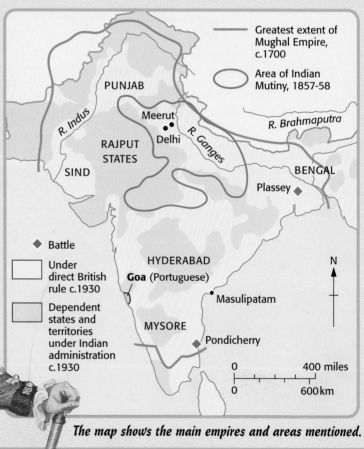

- —— Greatest extent of Mughal Empire, c.1700
- ⬭ Area of Indian Mutiny, 1857-58
- ◆ Battle
- ☐ Under direct British rule c.1930
- ☐ Dependent states and territories under Indian administration c.1930

PUNJAB
R. Indus
Meerut
Delhi
R. Ganges
R. Brahmaputra
RAJPUT STATES
SIND
BENGAL
Plassey
HYDERABAD
Goa (Portuguese)
Masulipatam
MYSORE
Pondicherry

N

| 0 | | 400 miles |
| 0 | | 600 km |

Robert Clive

The map shows the main empires and areas mentioned.

powerful south Indian state of Mysore. In 1803, the British seized the Mughal capital of Delhi, effectively ending Mughal power for good. The Marathas succumbed to British military might in 1823.

THE INDIAN MUTINY

As the 19th century progressed, the British conquered India's north-west regions, too. Sind was secured in 1843 and the Punjab, a Sikh stronghold, in 1849. Soon afterwards, however, this apparently unstoppable progress was temporarily halted by a serious rebellion.

The Indian Mutiny that broke out in 1857 had a major underlying cause, namely resistance to growing British influence. However, it was precipitated by the introduction of a new type of gun cartridge. A rumour quickly spread among the British-led Indian sepoys (soldiers) who had to use the cartridges that they were greased with pork or beef fat. Since Muslims considered pork to be unclean, and Hindus considered cows to be sacred, this was no small matter.

The mutiny began in Meerut, near Delhi, in May and soon 47 battalions were involved. So too were many civilians, making the uprising far more than just a military mutiny. By mid-June, the rebellion had spread across a great swathe of north-central India and in the following months, many Europeans were massacred. Delhi was retaken in September, but the mutiny was not quashed until July

A British viceroy and an Indian maharajah meet for talks.

1858. In the aftermath, another India Act was passed that gave all the East India Company's administrative powers to the British government and sovereign, Queen Victoria. The Raj – British rule – was now official.

LIFE UNDER THE RAJ

After India came under British government control in the 19th century, an elaborate hierarchy of officials was established to enforce London's rule. At its head was the Viceroy, the British monarch's representative in India. He was supported by thousands of civil servants, who sailed to India to administer even the farthest-flung corners of the sub-continent. In two-thirds of the country, British India proper, these men ruled

directly. In the rest, including the Rajput states of the north-west and the central Hyderabad region, they governed through local princes.

By the late 19th century, the Raj was fully established, and Anglo-Indians had developed a unique way of life. Civil servants often travelled to India with their families and set up Victorian-style households. In this they were supported by an array of Indian servants, including the *ayah* (maid), who looked after the *memsahib* (wife) and her children. In the summer, when the heat in the cities became unbearable, women and children often retired to cooler hill stations.

The British did not deliberately set out to make India's people change their existing ways of life. This was because London's main interest was not the transformation of society but the promotion of trade. Many settlers, however, set up new businesses such as tea, coffee and cotton plantations, as well as coal and iron mines. At the same time, railways were constructed to carry the goods produced to the coast for export. Unfortunately for India, the new steam trains also transported large quantities of British manufactured goods into the country, all but ruining its textile, glass-making and other industries as a result.

Elephants haul huge guns in this scene from the Indian Mutiny.

A NEW STRUGGLE

Gandhi sailed back into Mumbai in January 1915. Dressed in peasant's clothing, he was nevertheless greeted with much ceremony by the city's governor. After several more days of receptions, he and his family then travelled north to Gujarat. The time had come to begin a new struggle.

THE SATYAGRAHA ASHRAM

While returning from England in 1909 (see page 18), Gandhi had written a manifesto called *Hind Swaraj* ('Indian Home Rule'). It outlined his views on Indian independence, and made clear that he did not object to

Gandhi and his wife soon after their return home in 1915. In his autobiography, Gandhi wrote that it was a joy to get back to India.

British rule as such, but to the way it was corrupting Indian ways of life. Britain's introduction of mechanized industry and its emphasis on military might and material possessions were his major complaints. Now in India once again, Gandhi had the chance to act on these earlier ideas.

Gandhi's first major step, in May 1915, was to establish the Satyagraha ashram. As it was close to the Sabarmati River, near Ahmedabad, it was also known as the Sabarmati ashram. There he and about 200 other men and women were to live simply in Indian-village style. They were also to be celibate, own no personal possessions and eat no meat or rich foods. To demonstrate Gandhi's rejection of mechanized industry, ashram members made one further commitment – to wear only garments made of hand-spun cloth.

PREPARING FOR LEADERSHIP

Gandhi now involved himself increasingly in the work of the Indian National Congress, while at the same time travelling in third-class train carriages around the country to explain his ideas. He also concerned himself with the poor, particularly the untouchables (see page 28), whom he welcomed into his ashram. But despite all this activity, Gandhi did not have an official leadership role or a clear agenda with regard to the British, whose presence he was still prepared to tolerate.

Gandhi rose to greater prominence in 1917. During that year, he ran a successful campaign to end the emigration of indentured labourers to South Africa and led the first *satyagraha* protest in India. It occurred in Bihar, near Bengal, where English planters were exploiting local indigo-growers. Gandhi went to the state himself and persuaded its Lieutenant-Governor to set up an inquiry into the peasants' case. It found in their favour and obliged planters to compensate them.

In this scene from 1930, Gandhi is leading evening prayers at the Satyagraha ashram near Ahmedabad.

SATYAGRAHA STRUGGLES

In 1918, Gandhi stood alongside the poor once again, but this time closer to home, in Ahmedabad. One of the city's textile mills was owned by Ambalal Sarabhai, a supporter of Gandhi's ashram. During a 1917 plague outbreak, he had agreed to give his staff a 'plague bonus' for not fleeing the city but continuing to work. However, once the danger was over, he tried to avoid paying. He also refused to give workers the 35 per cent pay rise they were demanding, offering instead just 20 per cent.

Leading opposition to Ambalal was his sister, Anasuya, who asked Gandhi for support. He agreed to help her and the poor mill-workers lead a strike, provided they never resorted to violence or gave up. But after just three weeks, hunger and lack of pay began to shake the strikers' resolve. Then, however,

Gandhi introduced a new *satyagraha* tactic. On 15 March he began a fast, designed not to force Ambalal to negotiate, but to keep strikers true to their promise. Nevertheless, it did jolt the mill-owner into action, and a pay agreement was reached (see page 48).

Once the mill strike was over, Gandhi involved himself in another on behalf of Gujarati peasants in the Kheda (Kaira) district. A monsoon had drastically reduced their crop yields, and under such circumstances, regulations allowed them to postpone tax payments or not to make them at all. But the local British official was insisting on collecting the same amounts as usual. With Gandhi's support, the peasants refused to pay, but their stand won only a minor concession. In June 1918, the official agreed to suspend collection of taxes from the poorest farmers.

SUPPORTING THE EMPIRE

In the midst of the Kheda protests, in April 1918, Gandhi went to a conference in Delhi at the request of Lord Chelmsford, the

23

The Hindu Kumbh Mela festival is held in the Indian city of Hardwar every 12 years. In 1915, Gandhi went to the festival, where many pilgrims visited him to ask for advice.

Viceroy. By that time, Britain had been fighting the First World War for four years, and needed more men to take part in what would prove to be its final stages. At the conference, the Viceroy proposed a resolution asking for 500,000 Indian recruits to join the British army, and Gandhi publicly gave his support. But in an earlier letter accepting his invitation to the conference, he had made clear what he hoped for in return:

I recognize that, in the hour of its danger, we must give...ungrudging and unequivocal support to the Empire, of which we aspire, in the near future, to be partners in the same sense as the Dominions overseas. But it is the simple truth that our response is due to the expectation that our goal will be reached all the more speedily on that account...

THE ROWLATT ACTS

Gandhi not only supported the recruiting campaign, but played an active part in it. At the same time, he was eating a very restricted diet – just peanut butter and lemons – and the combination of hard work and inadequate food soon led to exhaustion, a nervous breakdown and a severe case of dysentery. He therefore had no option but to rest.

During Gandhi's illness, a British commission headed by Justice Rowlatt was inquiring into the use of terrorism and other violent methods by some campaigners for Indian home rule. The commission's report was published in July 1918. It suggested that rebels who stirred up opposition to the British, or who were even suspected of planning anti-government activities, should be tried in secret without the possibility of appeal, and should face severe penalties. The idea was to turn these proposals into laws, the Rowlatt Acts, as soon as possible.

Reaction to this plan was immediate and hostile. When Gandhi read a newspaper report about the proposed Acts, he was still a sick man. Nevertheless, he rallied his closest supporters around him and they all signed a pledge stating they would resist the new laws. Soon after, in Mumbai, Gandhi established the Satyagraha Sabha, an organization designed to co-ordinate nationwide protests if the laws came into effect. In addition, he travelled to Madras and other parts of India, explaining the purpose of the Acts and drumming up more opposition.

THE HARTAL

The British Viceroy and his officials paid little real attention to the storms of protest around them, and in March 1919 the Rowlatt Acts were passed. Early the following morning, Gandhi dreamed he should call a *hartal*, that is a general strike, to show that Indians simply would not obey the new laws. It took place on 30 March in Delhi, and 6 April in all other areas of India. Everywhere shops closed, factory machines ground to a halt and millions devoted themselves to fasting and prayer instead of work. Gandhi himself spent 6 April on the Mumbai seashore, where he was soon surrounded by an adoring crowd of some 150,000.

The *hartal* was another major turning point for Gandhi. The first Indian *satyagraha* organized for political purposes, it demonstrated that there was overwhelming support for defiance of the British government and ultimately home rule. It also proved Gandhi's power to motivate every section of Indian society, from the poorest Hindu untouchable to the wealthiest Muslim trader. He had first been dubbed 'Mahatma' ('great soul') back in 1915 by the famous Indian poet Rabindranath Tagore. But it was only after the *hartal* that the title was regularly used.

THE AMRITSAR MASSACRE

When the *hartal* was over, Gandhi set out on a trip, planning to visit first Delhi, then the Punjab region farther north. While he was on his way, however, disturbances broke out at several flashpoints, including Ahmedabad and Delhi itself. Fearing that Gandhi's presence in the capital would provoke yet more violence, the authorities arrested him and took him back to Mumbai. But this act, too, stirred up more unrest.

The bloodiest episode of this period occurred in Amritsar, a city in the Punjab holy to members of the Sikh religion (see page 29). On 13 April 1919, about 10,000 men gathered in an area of the city known as the Jallianwala Bagh to express opposition to the Rowlatt Acts. Such gatherings had been banned, so British army officer General Reginald Dyer ordered his Indian troops to fire, completely without warning, into the unarmed crowd. As many as 379 men were killed and 1,137 injured. Afterwards, the

THE CRAWLING ORDER

General Dyer is remembered not only for the 1919 Amritsar Massacre but also for an order that he issued soon after it took place. Following the tragedy, an English-woman working in India as a missionary was injured. Dyer therefore decreed that all Indians had to crawl rather than walk along the street where she lived. Soldiers were posted down the sides to make sure that everyone obeyed. Discussing all the cruelty that the British inflicted on Punjabis after the massacre, Gandhi wrote in his autobiography: 'Sentences were passed unwarranted by evidence and in flagrant violation of justice. In Amritsar innocent men and women were made to crawl like worms on their bellies. Before this outrage the Jallianwala Bagh tragedy paled into insignificance in my eyes...'

British introduced martial law and brutally repressed all dissent.

Gandhi was horrified at the violence that erupted in the aftermath of the *hartal*. So he fasted for three days as a penance, then on 19 April announced a temporary suspension of *satyagraha* opposition to the Rowlatt Acts. He also declared that his attempt to launch a *satyagraha* operation on such a huge scale without training more people in non-violent techniques was a 'Himalayan miscalculation'. Yet for all its disastrous results, the *hartal* did have one positive outcome: the British never put the Rowlatt Acts into practice.

TAKING CHARGE OF CONGRESS

Gandhi's attitude to the British altered irrevocably in 1919. Appalled by the Amritsar Massacre and the repression that followed, he felt he could no longer support any form of British presence in India. Millions of other Indians shared his view, and their disillusion

After the Amritsar Massacre, the British jailed hundreds of the city's people. Here, Indian prisoners are forced to file down the street.

was fuelled by disappointment. Britain had hinted that Indian participation in the First World War might bring greater self-government. However, after the British won the war in 1918 and the peace treaties were signed, little changed.

At this point, Gandhi began to play a much more active part in the Indian National Congress (see page 15). Previously, he had attended its meetings without much enthusiasm, but at the 1919 annual conference he became deeply involved in preparing its response to the events in Amritsar. Soon afterwards, he was asked to prepare a new constitution for the organization, and to alter its structure so that poor peasants and factory workers could participate more easily. (Until this time, most Congress members had been middle class, rich and highly educated.)

During this period, Gandhi also began to preach the idea of non-cooperation with the British. This proposal, which essentially involved boycotting British-run schools, courts, councils and more, was approved at the Indian National Congress's December 1920 conference in Nagpur. There the draft

By 1920, Gandhi had turned against British rule. So he returned the medals he had won in South Africa.

constitution Gandhi had prepared was also debated. It included a clear statement that Congress should work for *Swaraj* (home rule) within the British Empire if possible, but outside it if necessary. Muslims in the Congress very much wanted to remain in the Empire, but to their great distress the new constitution was adopted exactly as written.

Many other matters close to Gandhi's heart were also debated at Nagpur, and resolutions adopted to work for an end to untouchability (see page 28), to foster unity between Hindus and Muslims, and to promote simple village industries, particularly the hand-spinning of cloth. By the end of the discussions, Gandhi was clearly the dominant figure in Congress. Gokhale (see page 15) had died five years earlier in 1915, and Tilak in the summer of 1920. Gandhi was therefore able to take charge of the organization and lead it forwards in his own unique way.

Congress campaigns

The Indian National Congress had pledged itself to achieve *Swaraj* in 1921, so there was no time to lose. Gandhi himself criss-crossed India by train to promote non-cooperation with the British and participation in his 18-point 'constructive programme' to make the country ready for home rule. He asked men and women in villages everywhere to spin and wear *khadi* cloth, as he did, and to burn British-made textiles. He also encouraged people to educate themselves, and to speak Indian languages such as Hindi rather than English. Finally, he promoted basic hygiene, eagerly explaining the benefits of keeping both homes and streets clean.

Indians responded enthusiastically to Gandhi's campaign and throughout 1921, many lawyers, teachers, government officials and soldiers refused to co-operate with the authorities, or even stopped working altogether. Thousands were imprisoned as a result. However, not everyone followed the Mahatma's sacred principle of *ahimsa* (see page 7). When the Prince of Wales (the future King Edward VIII) visited the country, a *hartal* ordered by the Indian National Congress led to riots and deaths in Mumbai. In response, the British cracked down on the rebels and the dream of achieving home rule that year evaporated.

Crisis in Chauri Chaura

Gandhi remained a free man throughout all these upheavals, and in early 1922 prepared to begin a major new *satyagraha* operation. His intention was to encourage people not to pay their taxes, so that the British administration slowly collapsed through lack of money. Rather than launch this new tactic nationwide, however, Gandhi planned to begin in the Bardoli district, near Mumbai, then gradually introduce it elsewhere. The day set for the start of the campaign was 8 February.

Tragically, three days earlier, terrible violence erupted during a non-cooperation march in Chauri Chaura, a village in India's United Provinces some 400 kilometres from Bardoli. Twenty-two policemen were killed by the mob, then set alight. Disgusted, Gandhi at once called off the *satyagraha*. Just over a month later, on 10 March, the British arrested him for writing anti-government articles in a magazine called *Young India*. At the trial on 18 March, magistrate Robert Broomfield reluctantly sentenced Gandhi to six years in prison. This episode brought the first stage of his struggle for Indian home rule to an end.

THE RELIGIONS OF INDIA

Gandhi was a profoundly religious man born into a profoundly religious country. A Hindu himself (see page 6), he nevertheless acknowledged the truths to be found in many other faiths, declaring: 'Hinduism tells every one to worship God according to his own faith or dharma, and so it lives at peace with all religions.' On these two pages, you can learn a little about the central beliefs of all the major religions practised in India, and about how they affected Gandhi's own thoughts and actions.

HINDUISM

Hinduism developed about 4,500 years ago in the Indus Valley, an area now divided between north-west India and Pakistan. The faith was gradually carried into the rest of the sub-continent after a people known as the Aryans invaded northern India approximately 3,000 years ago.

Hindus believe in thousands of gods and goddesses, but also in a single great God, Brahman, who rules over them all. This supreme spirit is thought to have three forms – Brahma, the Creator, Vishnu, the Preserver, and Shiva, the Destroyer. Gandhi's family, and especially his mother, were devotees of Vishnu (see page 6).

Several other core beliefs unite all Hindus. First, they believe in samsara, a cycle of life and death during which a soul is reborn many times. Second, they believe in the law of karma. It teaches that people's actions in previous lives determine in what form their soul will return (for example as an animal or a person), as well as what will happen in their new lives. Finally Hindus believe in dharma, a moral code that, if properly followed, will enable them to break out of the samsara cycle and so attain moksha, that is reunion with Brahman.

Hindus also accept the caste system. It divides them into four hereditary classes (castes) known as Brahmans (priests), Kshatriyas (warriors), Vaisyas (merchants) and Sudras (farmers and peasants), as well as a fifth group, the untouchables. These people were considered unclean and shunned

The Bhagavad Gita, a Hindu holy book, greatly influenced Gandhi.

by the rest of society, but Gandhi called them *Harijan* (children of God) and tried to end their plight.

The 16th-century Mughal emperor Akbar (seated, centre).

ISLAM

Islam was founded by the Prophet Muhammad in Arabia during the 7th century AD and was first brought to India soon afterwards. From the 11th to the 13th centuries, Muslim sultanates ruled Delhi. The Mughal emperors (see page 20) later strengthened the faith's position in India, although the greatest of these rulers, such as Emperor Akbar (1542–1605), tolerated other religions, too.

Islam has one holy book, the Qur'an, and one central belief, namely that: 'There is no God but Allah and Muhammad is his Prophet.' Muslims are obliged to spread this message, and in centuries past found willing converts among untouchable and low-caste Hindus, to whom the new faith offered an escape route from the rigid caste system. But Islam never replaced Hinduism as the religion of the Indian majority.

Gandhi believed that of all the great world faiths, Islam 'most beautifully' expressed the ideas of monotheism and equality. He also struggled to create a united India where Muslims and Hindus could live together in peace. He therefore considered Partition (see page 39) to be a 'spiritual tragedy', and on Independence Day (see page 41) did not attend official celebrations in Delhi. Instead, he went to Calcutta to fast, pray and visit Muslims whose homes had been attacked by Hindu mobs.

SIKHISM

Sikhism was founded in India during the 15th century AD by a guru called Nanak. Growing out of Hinduism, it incorporated beliefs such as the cycle of death and rebirth. However, it rejected polytheism and the caste system, maintaining instead that there is only one God and that all people are of equal worth. At first, Sikhs also opposed violence.

After Nanak died, he was followed by a succession of nine other gurus. They turned away from pacifism, and by the 18th century, Sikh men were known for their military skills. After Gobind Singh, the 10th guru, died in 1708, there were no more of these spiritual leaders. So instead of relying on the teachings of living

Buddhism began in India but by Gandhi's time was not much practised there.

individuals, Sikhs began to consult the *Adi Granth Sahib*, their holy book. It contains not only the words of the gurus, but also some Hindu and Muslim scriptures.

Gandhi considered that Sikhism was not a different faith from Hinduism, but rather an adaptation of it. He was impressed by the high ethical values and spirituality of the *Adi Granth Sahib*, but could accept neither the militarism nor the meat-eating of Sikh culture.

CHRISTIANITY

Christianity arrived in India from the Middle East during the 1st century AD. The faith's earliest stronghold was Kerala, on the south-west coast. However Goa, further to the north, also became a Christian centre after it was colonized by the Roman Catholic Portuguese in 1510.

Gandhi was not impressed by the Christian missionaries who came to India with the British (see page 20), but while in England was persuaded to read the Bible. He found much of the Old Testament boring, but the New Testament was a revelation. Gandhi later wrote that its depiction of the life and teachings of Jesus Christ, whom Christians believe to be the Son of God, 'went straight to my heart'. This was particularly true of the Sermon on the Mount, in which Jesus preaches non-violence, saying: 'Do not resist an evil person. If someone strikes you on the right cheek, turn to him the other also.' Gandhi also admired Christianity's emphasis on God as a loving Father.

Despite his appreciation of Christianity, and the best efforts of his friends in South Africa (see page 14), Gandhi was never seriously tempted to convert. Yet in a 1946 prayer meeting, he readily declared: 'I think I am as much a Christian, a Sikh and a Jain as I am a Hindu.'

The Golden Temple in the Punjabi city of Amritsar is the Sikhs' most holy shrine.

29

CHAPTER FOUR

TOWARDS INDEPENDENCE

Gandhi spent his jail term (see page 27) in Yeravda Prison near the city of Pune in north-west India. He did not find the experience an ordeal, but rather appreciated the free time that it gave him to meditate, read, write and spin. However, this interlude ended much more quickly than Gandhi had anticipated. After he developed appendicitis in early 1924, he was taken to a local hospital for an operation. When he was slow to recover, it was decided that he should be released on 5 February.

CONGRESS IN CRISIS

India's political situation had changed greatly since 1922. In particular, the Indian National Congress now contained two groups that were pursuing home rule in different ways. One group wanted to participate in British-approved legislative councils that would give Indians some political influence, while allowing them to fight for dominion status (self-governing status within the British Empire) from inside the system. In 1922, it had set up the Swaraj Party to campaign for election to the councils. The other group wished to continue complete, Gandhi-style non-cooperation.

Faced with such disarray and his own supporters' reluctance to begin large-scale *satyagraha* protests once again, Gandhi decided to turn aside from politics, at least temporarily. Instead he planned to return to his 'constructive programme' of strengthening India at grass-roots level (see page 27). Nevertheless, the circumstances of the next few months prevented him withdrawing completely from the political arena.

HINDU-MUSLIM TENSIONS

In the wider world, the always fragile unity between Hindus and Muslims had begun to collapse. A particular cause of friction was Muslims' killing and eating of cows, animals

About 20 Hindus and 11 Muslims were killed in the Kohat riots of 1924. This was the scene of devastation on the riots' second day.

that Hindus believed to be holy. Hindus meanwhile angered Muslims by processing and playing music in front of mosques during prayer times. There were other, underlying causes of unrest, too, particularly the fact that Hindus generally had access to better education and jobs than Muslims.

In autumn 1924, tensions in the North-West Province town of Kohat exploded into violence and many people were massacred. Horrified, on 18 September Gandhi began a 21-day fast designed to encourage the rebuilding of relationships between the two warring communities. This had only limited success, but it proved Gandhi's willingless to sacrifice his health, even his life, to the cause. In December 1924, Gandhi again disregarded his personal well-being by agreeing to serve as Congress president. He did not really want the post, but felt he should use his skills to hold the ailing organization together.

A YEAR'S RETREAT

As he had wished, and despite his new appointment, Gandhi devoted little time to political pursuits in 1925. Instead he travelled the length and breadth of India, talking to thousands of people and promoting *khadi* cloth. His audiences treated him with great reverence, delighted simply to hear the words, and if possible touch the feet, of the much-loved Mahatma.

In December 1925, Gandhi resigned as President of the Indian National Congress and vowed to observe 'political silence' for the next year. Now he retreated to the Satyagraha ashram and spent his time working, praying, talking to admirers who visited from around the world, and writing letters and magazine articles. On Mondays he did not speak at all, but used the time for spiritual contemplation. Occasionally, however, he would scribble important messages on pieces of paper.

THE SIMON COMMISSION

In accordance with his plans, Gandhi left the ashram again in December 1926 and resumed his travels around India. But then, on 26 October 1927, he received a summons that was to prompt his return to full-time political campaigning. It came from Lord Irwin, Viceroy of India, and requested Gandhi's attendance at a meeting in Delhi on 5 November.

In fact, several leading Indians had been called to meet Lord Irwin, and gathered at the appointed time. There was no discussion, however. Instead, the Viceroy simply handed out a document explaining that a British commission led by Sir John Simon would soon arrive in India. Its role was to investigate the situation in the country, and suggest political

The Simon Commission (in light-coloured suits and hats) on arrival in India. Sir John Simon himself is third from the left.

reforms. It was to include not a single Indian representative and would present its conclusions only to the British parliament back in London.

Gandhi was outraged at the complete disregard for the wishes of the Indian people that this new move represented. So he made up his mind there and then to oppose the Commission in whatever way he could. The Indian National Congress, the Muslim League and millions of ordinary Indians, Hindu and Muslim alike, also decided to resist the British plan. A new and powerful wave of protests was about to begin.

THE BARDOLI REVOLT

When the Simon Commission arrived in Mumbai on 3 February 1928, it was greeted by Indians waving black flags and shouting that its members should go home. Once it set to work, it was boycotted by Gandhi and every other Indian with any power. No one would give evidence or provide information, so it was hard for the seven-person team to compile an accurate report. While they tried, Gandhi launched a new *satyagraha*.

The location for this protest was Bardoli, where the 1922 tax revolt was to have taken place (see page 27). Now, on 12 February 1928, Gandhi launched the revolt for real, and soon 87,000 peasants were refusing to pay their taxes. The British responded by arresting hundreds of them, driving many more off their land, and seizing the animals that they used to draw ploughs and provide milk. The peasants, however, stood firm and, to Gandhi's relief, also remained non-violent.

The situation in Bardoli attracted the attention of Indians all over the country, and on 12 June they staged a nationwide *hartal* in support of the participants. At first, the British authorities refused to budge. But then, on 6 August, they capitulated. All the people who had been arrested were set free and a commission was established that eventually agreed to the tax cuts the protesters had

demanded. Meanwhile, peasants' animals and land were returned or compensation for them paid.

A FATEFUL YEAR

The success of the Bardoli *satyagraha* stirred up the atmosphere of rebellion throughout India. As a result, the December 1928 Indian National Congress meeting in Calcutta was turbulent. Some hot-headed young members pressed for an immediate declaration of independence, but fearing this would cause violence, Gandhi urged caution. Accepting his advice, Congress passed a resolution demanding dominion status for India within a year. Even Gandhi proclaimed that if no progress had been made by then, he would campaign for complete independence.

During 1929, Viceroy Lord Irwin indicated that he was seriously considering Congress's request. However, London politicians of several parties forced him to backtrack. As a result, when Congress met in Lahore in December, the mood was defiant. Britain had been obstinate and treacherous. The only way forward therefore was to demand total independence outside its empire. A resolution to this effect was duly adopted. Then new Congress president Jawaharlal Nehru asked Gandhi to lead a comprehensive *satyagraha* designed to force the British out.

THE SALT SATYAGRAHA

On 26 January 1930, Gandhi published the 'Indian Declaration of Independence'. After outlining the disastrous effects of British rule on India, it proclaimed: 'We believe…that India must sever the British connection and attain *Purna Swaraj*, or Complete Independence.' However, Gandhi was not yet ready to begin the *satyagraha* that would play a large part in achieving this aim. First, he had carefully to choose its target.

Everyone needs some salt in their diet, but this is especially true in hot countries such as India, where much of this vital substance is lost from the body in perspiration. Seeing a chance for raising money, the British had imposed a tax on salt and made it illegal for Indians to prepare it for nothing from sea water. This tax hit the poor hardest, as most of them did heavy physical labour that made them sweat. Gandhi eventually decided that his new *satyagraha* would be directed against the salt tax. The start date for the protests was to be 12 March 1930.

As dawn broke on that day, the 60-year-old Gandhi and 78 of his followers set out on foot from the Satyagraha ashram. Their destination

On 6 April 1930, Gandhi picked up a handful of salt in the coastal town of Dandi. This symbolic gesture brought turmoil to India.

was the coastal town of Dandi, 150 kilometres to the south, which they planned to reach in about three weeks. All along the way, villagers came out to greet the Mahatma and threw branches in front of him to make the path softer for his feet. In the evenings, they listened, too, as he talked about his dreams of a better future for India. Many villagers also joined the procession, wishing to play their part in making that dream a reality.

The marchers, now numbering several thousand, reached Dandi on 5 April. The following morning, they swam in the ocean, then made their way ashore. Next, Gandhi stooped to pick up a handful of salt that the retreating waves had left behind. This small, simple and illegal act ignited extraordinary passions across India. In clear defiance of the British authorities, thousands of people who lived near the sea's edge went there to collect salt for themselves. They were all unceremoniously arrested.

Much more agitation followed, as other Indians set out to disrupt British rule. Local leaders and members of legislative councils resigned, or made public readings of anti-government literature. There were also many demonstrations against shops that sold foreign cloth. Unusually, thousands of women, some breaking *purdah* for the first time, played an active part. Almost all the protesters maintained *ahimsa*. However the police, who arrested a total of 60,000 people, were often brutal.

CONFRONTATION AT DHARASANA

Many Congress leaders, including Jawaharlal Nehru, were among those imprisoned during the salt tax protests. Gandhi, however, remained a free man and now began planning the invasion of factories where the British authorities made salt. But on 4 May, while he was asleep under a mango tree, a British magistrate and 30 Indian policemen came to arrest him. He had no choice but to go with them and was soon in prison again.

The scene outside the Dharasana Salt Works in May 1930. Indian protesters are already in rows ready to advance on the compound.

Despite this setback, Gandhi's followers saw no reason to abandon their plans. So on 21 May, 2,500 of them set out for the Dharasana Salt Works, some 250 kilometres north of Mumbai. At their head was poet Mrs Sarojini Naidu, who had stood alongside Gandhi at the dramatic conclusion of the Salt March. The Dharasana Works was guarded by 400 Indian policemen, led by six British officers. When the protesters arrived, the police blocked their way, brandishing steel-plated wooden sticks.

The protesters, led by Gandhi's son Manilal, then began to advance in silent rows. As each man reached the police guard, he was beaten about the head, and the terrible sound of wood on bone filled the air. And as each man fell, his head bloody and often his skull fractured, another grimly moved up to take his place. Meanwhile the women dragged the broken bodies away. In accordance with *ahimsa*, the protesters offered no violence in return for the violence that they received. By the end of the day, two of them were dead and 320 injured.

News of events in Dharasana quickly spread around the globe – a shocking account by American reporter Webb Miller appeared in over 1,000 different newspapers. The story provoked great praise for the courage of the protesters, but harsh condemnation of the British officers who had ordered such brutality against them. In an article in British newspaper the *Manchester Guardian*, Rabindranath Tagore (see page 25) summed up the widespread reaction with these words: 'Europe has completely lost her former moral prestige in Asia...'

THE ROUND TABLE CONFERENCE

Non-cooperation continued for the rest of the year, and by its end some 100,000 protesters were in jail. Realizing that the situation could not be allowed to continue, British Prime Minister Ramsay MacDonald urged the Viceroy to act. So on 26 January 1931, Lord Irwin released Gandhi, Nehru and other Congress leaders from prison. Then the Mahatma and the Viceroy held meetings in Delhi that led to the Irwin-Gandhi Pact of 5 March. In it, Gandhi agreed to end the *satyagraha*, while Irwin agreed to free protesters still in jail, and to let Indians make salt for private use.

The Pact contained one other important provision: Gandhi was to represent the Indian National Congress at the Round Table Conference on his country's future shortly to take place in London. Sailing from Mumbai on 29 August, Gandhi arrived in England two weeks later and made his temporary home in

Wearing his usual, home-spun clothing, Gandhi sits alongside Indians and Englishmen in more formal dress at the Round Table Conference.

London's East End, among the poor. The conference itself, however, was held in the much grander environment of St James's Palace, a royal residence in the centre of the city.

Gandhi was one of 96 conference participants from India. They ranged from maharajahs to untouchables, and were divided by wealth, way of life and religion. Sadly, each was so concerned to ensure that his own group was properly represented in any new Indian government that the issue of independence itself faded into the background. Even Gandhi, who spoke for more Indians than any other delegate, found it difficult to make his voice heard. As a result, little of substance was achieved.

The failure of the Round Table Conference was to have lasting effects. Instead of fostering the strong, unified India for which Gandhi so fervently wished, it intensified the divisions between Hindus, Muslims, Sikhs and others. In the last years of the independence struggle, these divisions were to grow only deeper and more bitter.

A LANCASHIRE WELCOME

During his three-month stay in England, Gandhi took the opportunity to visit the northern county of Lancashire, where textile-making was a major industry. There he met many poor cotton-mill workers (see right) who had lost their jobs because of his opposition to British cloth in India. Far from rejecting him, however, these people welcomed him warmly and listened attentively to his accounts of the terrible poverty in his home country. One man even declared: 'I am one of the unemployed, but if I was in India, I would say the same thing that Mr Gandhi is saying.'

CHAPTER FIVE

THE FINAL YEARS

Gandhi returned to India on 28 December 1931. During his absence, a new Viceroy, Lord Willingdon, had taken over and introduced harsh measures to crush resistance and to restrict the power of the Indian National Congress. Jawaharlal Nehru (see page 32) had already been jailed and on 4 January 1932, Gandhi was likewise put behind bars.

A FATAL FAST?

Back in Yeravda Prison (see page 30), Gandhi was quite at ease. But then one issue began to cause him great concern. The British were in the process of devising a new Indian constitution, and intended to put the untouchables into a different electorate from other Hindus. In other words, they were to make up a separate category of voters and to elect their own

Beggars outside the Kalighat Temple, Calcutta. After Gandhi's campaigns, the temple was opened to untouchables for the first time.

separate delegates. Gandhi considered this to be immoral, since it seemed to reinforce the untouchables' supposed inferior status.

Gandhi now proclaimed he would stop eating if the British went ahead, and began his fast to the death on 20 September 1932. At once untouchables, caste Hindus and Muslims sought a solution that would save his life. Eventually, a compromise, the Yeravda Pact, was reached. On 26 September, Gandhi broke his fast by drinking some orange juice.

The end of the fast did not mean the end of Gandhi's commitment to the untouchables. On the contrary, he now devoted himself to their cause, even founding a society for the purpose. Then in November 1933, six months after his release from jail, he began a 19,000-kilometre trip around India to help raise money for the *Harijan* (see page 28). Many Hindus responded sympathetically – sharing food with untouchables, or allowing them in temples where they had been banned.

RURAL IMPROVEMENT

In October 1934, Gandhi withdrew from the Indian National Congress, believing he should again concentrate on building up Indian village life. To this end, he founded the All-India Village Industries Association, which promoted spinning and other skills, supported schemes to improve education, sanitation, medical care and diet, and campaigned for the rights of women, whom Gandhi believed were men's equals. In 1936, Gandhi moved from his home in north-west India to the central Deccan area. There he set up a new ashram that he called Sevagram. It became the centre of his rural improvement campaigns.

POLITICAL CHANGE

While Gandhi was devoting himself to rural life, a major political change had taken place. In October 1935, Britain's parliament had passed the Government of India Act, which allowed Indians to rule themselves at provincial but not national level. (The country was then divided into 11 provinces.) Gandhi was highly sceptical about this development, which left Britain firmly in overall charge.

The chance for more fundamental change arrived after the Second World War (1939–1945) had begun. Although India now had elected provincial governments, Viceroy Lord Linlithgow did not consult them before taking the country into the fighting on the British side. The Indian National Congress responded by offering to support Britain only if India were granted more independence. Gandhi deplored both the war and attempts to bargain over India's participation. But in late 1939, he agreed to present Congress's requests to the Viceroy.

The Viceroy refused to accept the deal that Congress offered, so its members refused to help Britain. In addition, Congress ministers in provincial governments resigned. The stand-off continued into 1940, while Germany, Britain's main war enemy, was winning major victories in Europe. Finally in July, hoping to make the most of British weakness, Congress demanded full independence. But Winston Churchill, Britain's new Prime Minister, dismissed the idea with contempt.

A NEW APPROACH

Throughout this period, Gandhi had maintained his total commitment to non-violence. Having failed to make progress towards independence by offering to join the war, Congress now turned to him for advice. From October 1940, at his suggestion, Indian politicians and others began to speak out against the fighting, in defiance of British regulations. Within 14 months, more than 23,000 of these protesters had been arrested.

Gandhi's campaign failed to break Britain's resolve. But then, on 7 December 1941, the Japanese launched an air raid on an American naval base in Pearl Harbor, Hawaii. This attack marked Japan's entry into the Second World War on Germany's side, and prompted the USA's entry on Britain's side. Soon there was fighting all around the Pacific Ocean, near India, and British colonies in the Far East were falling to Japan.

Other developments also caused a change in Britain's attitude towards India. From 1942, Winston Churchill led a special wartime coalition government, many of whose members were sympathetic to the idea of Indian independence. So, too, was US President Roosevelt, who urged the Prime Minister to find a lasting solution to the subcontinent's difficulties. Eventually, Churchill decided that he had to act. Personally, he had no wish to see Indian independence, but he needed both Indian and American support in the war.

QUIT INDIA

The man Churchill now selected to deal with the question of Indian home rule was Sir Stafford Cripps, a distinguished Labour member of the government. He arrived in Delhi in March 1942, then presented Britain's new proposals. Indian leaders soon rejected them.

Among Gandhi's many objections was the fact that any of India's 11 provinces could choose not to join the independent country that the plans would create.

Cripps left India on 12 April. Despite his failure, Britain insisted that its proposals for Indian home rule could not be altered. The Indian National Congress therefore took matters into its own hands, and on 8 August 1942 adopted a historic resolution. This stated that the British should 'Quit India' at once. If they did not, a new *satyagraha* campaign would begin under Gandhi's leadership. Soon afterwards, Gandhi, Nehru and other Congress leaders were arrested once more.

The arrests triggered outbreaks of violence across India. Symbols of British authority such as government offices were burned down, and many people were killed. Lord Linlithgow, the Viceroy at the time, blamed Gandhi for the chaos. In protest at such an unjust interpretation of the facts, the Mahatma engaged in another 21-day fast that nearly cost him his life.

A GREAT LOSS

Gandhi's wife, Kasturbai, was imprisoned the day after him in the summer of 1942. In late 1943, still in jail, she developed severe bronchitis. Doctors' efforts to cure her proved fruitless and Gandhi banned the use of penicillin – he did not approve of injections. Kasturbai died on 22 February 1944, with Gandhi by her side. Afterwards he declared:

This map shows the movements of Hindu and Muslim refugees between India and Pakistan (East and West) at the time of independence.

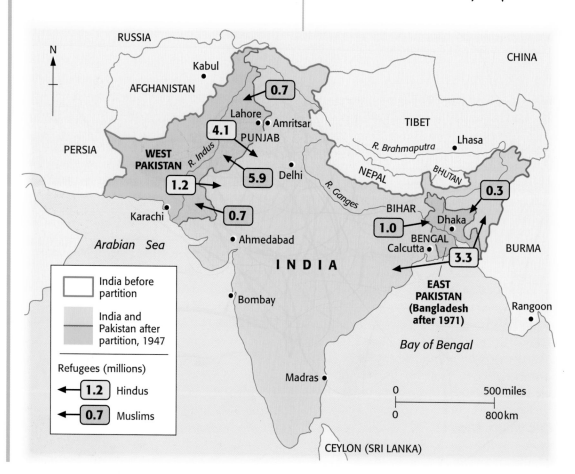

38

'Her passing has left a vacuum which never will be filled.'

Soon after Kasturbai's death, Gandhi's own health took a turn for the worse – he developed first malaria, then anaemia – and thousands of Indians clamoured for him to be released. Fearing terrible violence if the Mahatma were to die in prison, new Viceroy Lord Wavell gave his permission and Gandhi regained his freedom on 6 May 1944.

UNITY OR PARTITION?

The final push for India's freedom began in 1945, after Britain and its allies had won the Second World War. The conditions were now right in London, where a new Labour government led by Clement Attlee was in favour of Indian independence. They were right in India, too, where the British authorities, weary of war, had no appetite for more conflict.

After Attlee's government had officially committed itself to self-rule for India, elections were held in the country and both the Indian National Congress and Muslim League (see page 15) won many seats in the legislative councils. However, there was no agreement between Britain and India over the form post-independence government should take. Hindus and Muslims were increasingly at odds over the issue, too.

While Congress members had been in prison, the Muslim League had grown in strength. Its leader, Muhammad Ali Jinnah (see box), did not share Gandhi's vision of a single India where people of all faiths could live together. Instead he favoured the establishment of a separate Muslim state called Pakistan, where the sub-continent's 100 million Muslim minority would not be dominated by its 300 million Hindus. Many other Muslims had taken this idea of Partition to their hearts.

THE CABINET MISSION

To discover the best way forward, Britain sent a Cabinet Mission to Delhi in March 1946.

MUHAMMAD ALI JINNAH

Muhammad Ali Jinnah (below) was born in 1876, in Gandhi's home state of Gujarat. Like Gandhi, he studied law in London, but unlike him was then able to establish a successful legal practice in India. As a young Muslim man, Jinnah became an active member of the Indian National Congress, and was as fervently in favour of a united India as Gandhi. But after participating in the 1931 Round Table Conference (see pages 34–35), he became convinced that Muslims could never escape Hindu domination under such circumstances. Disheartened, he therefore remained in Britain for some years. In 1934, shortly after his return to India, he became President of the Muslim League, and in that role successfully fought for Partition. In 1947, Jinnah was made the first governor-general of Pakistan, a post he retained until his death in 1948.

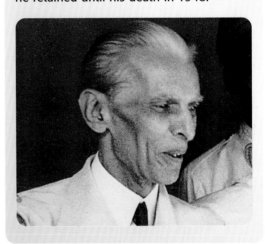

After much consultation with the Indian National Congress and the Muslim League, the Cabinet Mission published a proposal in May. This document rejected Partition for two main reasons: first, millions of Muslims did not live within the borders of the proposed state of Pakistan, while millions of Hindus did, and second, Pakistan's division into two areas separated by India (see map page 38) was highly impractical.

Angry at this development, Jinnah refused to participate in the provisional government that the British had asked Jawaharlal Nehru to form. Then, on 16 August, the Muslim League held a 'Direct Action Day' in favour of a separate Pakistan that led to great Hindu-Muslim violence. On 2 September, Nehru became Prime Minister of India, and soon after, Muslim League members joined his provisional government. However, the signs for a peaceful future were not good.

Throughout the autumn, tension between Hindus and Muslims grew, and led to much bloodshed. After many Hindus were killed in East Bengal, Gandhi felt he had to intervene. So he made his way to the region, then walked from village to village, reconciling people through prayer and preaching. In March 1947, after calm had been restored, Gandhi went to Bihar, where Hindus had killed thousands of Muslims.

THE ROAD TO INDEPENDENCE

Meanwhile, the political discussions about India's future were continuing, and Partition remained a stumbling block. As the prospect of civil war loomed, Attlee (see page 39) decided simply to announce a date for British withdrawal from the country. So on 20 February 1947, he declared that it would take place no later than June 1948. He also made known that a new Viceroy, Lord Louis Mountbatten, would oversee the process.

Mountbatten arrived in Delhi in March, then began discussions with both Jinnah and Gandhi. It soon became clear that Jinnah would never accept a united India, and that further delay in recognizing that fact would only make civil war more likely. On that basis, Mountbatten persuaded Congress, though not Gandhi, to agree to Partition. Jinnah had to make concessions, too, however. He wanted all of the Bengal and Punjab provinces to become part of Pakistan. But

Nehru was prime minister of India from 1947 to 1964. At the start of his time in office, India was a British dominion. But in 1950, it became a fully independent republic.

Gandhi with Lord Louis Mountbatten and his wife, Edwina.

40

because they had large Hindu populations, Lord Mountbatten insisted that they be divided, too.

Lord Mountbatten's independence plan was announced in both Britain and India on 3 June 1947, and the Indian National Congress soon gave it their official approval. However, the fact that India and Pakistan were to be separate dominions filled Gandhi with sorrow. When Independence Day arrived on 15 August 1947, he did not join the Delhi celebrations, but spent the day helping Muslim victims of Hindu violence in Calcutta.

MORE VIOLENCE

At first, Gandhi brought calm to Calcutta, but then trouble flared up again. Aiming to bring people to their senses, the Mahatma began a fast to the death on 1 September. At once, Hindus and Muslims urgently sought a way to end the fighting, and three days later presented Gandhi with a written pledge that it would stop. He therefore began to eat again.

Tragically, although peace was restored in Calcutta, much of the rest of India was in turmoil. As millions of Hindus made their way from Pakistan to India, and millions of Muslims did the reverse (see page 38), a wave of violence swept the country. The Punjab region, now divided between India and Pakistan, was especially badly hit.

THE FINAL FAST

Thousands of refugees from the bloodshed made their way to Delhi, which was itself torn by strife. After his Calcutta fast was over, Gandhi, too, went there and settled in a building called Birla House. He then spent his days helping the refugees in any way that he could, and every evening held a multi-faith prayer meeting in the grounds of his home.

Gandhi's efforts restored a measure of peace to Delhi, but Hindu resentment against Muslims there remained strong. As so often before, the Mahatma decided that he would fast to the death in an attempt to bring

'a reunion of hearts of all communities'. Now a 78-year-old man, he stopped eating on 13 January 1948, and soon grew weak. Distressed by his frailty, leaders of Delhi's religious communities tried to solve their differences. Eventually, they signed a pledge promising an end to violence, and on 18 January the Mahatma took nourishment again.

DEATH OF THE MAHATMA

Revived by the success of his fast, which also helped bring calm to the rest of India, Gandhi resumed his routine of ending the day with a prayer meeting outside Birla House. On 20 January, a Hindu who believed Gandhi was too tolerant of Muslims threw a bomb into the grounds. The Mahatma was not hurt and the man was quickly arrested.

Another Hindu extremist, Nathuram Godse, now took his chance. On 30 January 1948, he joined the crowd waiting for Gandhi to begin his evening prayer meeting. As the Mahatma approached, Godse shot him several times. Gandhi at once fell to the ground, the word Rama (Hindi for 'God') on his lips. He died in seconds. After his funeral, his ashes were scattered where the holy Jumna and Ganges rivers meet.

Gandhi's body was publicly cremated on the banks of the Jumna river the day after his death. His pyre burned for 14 hours.

JUDGE
FOR YOURSELF

SAINT OR POLITICIAN?

During his lifetime, people found it difficult to classify Gandhi. To his followers, he was a holy man, a mahatma, or even an avatar (god in human form). But to his many critics in Britain and India, he was a wily operator prepared to use religion as a cover for his efforts to win Indian independence and reform Indian society. Some also considered that his personal behaviour did not always match up to the high standards that he set. So was Gandhi a saint, a politician, or a mixture of the two? Read both sides of the argument and the sources, then judge for yourself.

SAINT?

SOURCE 1

The outstanding impression my mother has left on my memory is that of saintliness. She was deeply religious. She would not think of taking her meals without her daily prayers. Going to [the temple dedicated to the god Vishnu] was one of her daily duties...
(EXTRACT FROM *AN AUTOBIOGRAPHY* BY M.K. GANDHI)

SOURCE 2

47 Set thy heart upon thy work, but never on its reward. Work not for a reward; but never cease to do thy work.
(EXTRACT FROM CHAPTER TWO OF *THE BHAGAVAD GITA*)

SOURCE 3

A Christian enters into no dispute with his neighbour, he neither attacks nor uses violence; on the contrary, he suffers himself, without resistance...
(EXTRACT FROM *THE KINGDOM OF GOD IS WITHIN YOU* BY LEO TOLSTOY)

A GUIDING PRINCIPLE

Gandhi grew up in a home where religion was taken very seriously, especially by his mother (*Source 1*). However, he studied Hinduism only after arriving in London in 1888. Reading the *Bhagavad Gita* (see page 28), he was impressed by the idea that people should act morally without thought of reward, and it became a guiding principle of his life (*Source 2*).

DEVELOPING BELIEFS

In South Africa from 1893, Gandhi learned more about many faiths. Having studied the Bible in London, he now read *The Kingdom of God Is Within You*. The emphasis on non-violence in this Christian work by Russian writer Leo Tolstoy (*Source 3*) was an inspiration. Of course, religious knowledge is not the same as saintliness. But now Gandhi acted on his developing beliefs, and his saintly nature started to become clear.

FAITH IN ACTION

After first becoming a rich lawyer in South Africa, Gandhi began to devote himself to the struggle for racial justice. He also discarded the trappings of success, choosing instead the simple life he read about in John Ruskin's *Unto This Last* (see page 17 and *Source 4*). As part of this process, he set up

John Ruskin (1819-1900)

both Phoenix and Tolstoy Farms, and took his *brahmacharya* vow, committing himself to a life of saintly self-control.

A SINGLE PURPOSE

After returning to India in 1915, Gandhi continued his simple lifestyle. At home in the Satyagraha ashram (see page 22), he lived frugally in one small room. In the wider world, he helped the poor tirelessly, for example during the Ahmedabad textile strike

Gandhi's simple room and spinning wheel in the Satyagraha ashram.

(see page 23). To him, practical as well as more obviously spiritual activities like prayer all had one main purpose: to help an individual draw nearer to God (*Source 5*).

THE FIGHT FOR INDEPENDENCE

Gandhi's role in India's independence struggle provides more evidence of his saintliness. His insistence on non-violence during *satyagraha* protests, and his willingness to fast to the death to end violence (see page 41), mark him out as a special kind of man. In accordance with the teachings of the *Bhagavad Gita*, he would use only moral means to achieve his aims, and was ready to sacrifice his life if necessary.

BEYOND POLITICS

Gandhi's support for the untouchables (see page 28) is another reason to believe his inspiration was spiritual not worldly, since it brought him no real political gain. His 'constructive programme' for village India (see page 27) also proved his commitment to the poor. On a personal level, Gandhi's extreme kindness and patience to all were legendary.

AN INDIAN SAINT

It is self-evident that Gandhi involved himself deeply in politics. But he did so not as a man for whom either the pursuit of power or the simple wish to do good was the driving force. Rather he served the Indian people as a spiritual duty and with a spiritual purpose. He was therefore no ordinary politician but an Indian saint (*Sources 6* and 7).

SOURCE 4

[People should seek] *not greater wealth, but simpler pleasure; not higher fortune but deeper felicity* [happiness]*; making the first of possessions, self-possession; and honouring themselves in the harmless pride and calm pursuits of peace.*
(EXTRACT FROM *UNTO THIS LAST* BY JOHN RUSKIN)

SOURCE 5

I count no sacrifice too great for the sake of seeing God face to face. The whole of my activity, whether it may be called social, political, humanitarian or ethical, is directed to that end...
(EXTRACT FROM *MY PHILOSOPHY OF LIFE* EDITED BY ANAND T. HINGORANI)

SOURCE 6

The politician in me has never dominated a single decision of mine, and if I seem to take part in politics, it is only because politics encircle us today like the coil of a snake from which one cannot get out, no matter how much one tries.
(EXTRACT FROM AN ARTICLE BY GANDHI IN *YOUNG INDIA*)

SOURCE 7

Gandhi saw himself first as a seeker after religious Truth, for whom the realm of social involvement was a means to further his own spiritual liberation.
(EXTRACT FROM 'GANDHI'S MORAL PHILOSOPHY' BY STEVEN A. SMITH)

SAINT OR POLITICIAN?

POLITICIAN?

SOURCE 8

...without his being committed to a normal course of life by child marriage, he might well have been a monastic saint instead of what he became: politician and reformer with an honorary sainthood. For the true saints are those who transfer the state of householdership [building a family and home] *to the house of God, becoming father and mother, brother and sister, son and daughter, to all creation...*
(EXTRACT FROM *GANDHI'S TRUTH* BY ERIK H. ERIKSON)

SOURCE 9

[Satyagraha resistance] *is a force which, if it became universal, would revolutionize social ideals and do away with despotisms and the ever-growing militarism under which the nations of the West are groaning and are being almost crushed to death, and which fairly promises to overwhelm even the nations of the East.*
(EXTRACT FROM THE NEWSPAPER *INDIAN OPINION*)

PUBLIC STRUGGLES

Gandhi's devotion to religious ideals cannot be doubted. Nevertheless, first in South Africa and later in India, it was as a politician that he made his mark. Though his personal faith was a constant backdrop, the greater part of Gandhi's life was devoted to public struggles with both national and local governments in an effort to improve all Indians' lives.

POLITICAL APPRENTICESHIP

In his famous book about Gandhi, psychoanalyst Erik H. Erikson suggests that, but for his early marriage, the Mahatma might have chosen a life of celibate sainthood (*Source 8*). However once he had married, in 1882, he felt that he had to remain loyal. Gandhi's political apprenticeship began later, in South Africa. There he both discovered his gift for winning the devotion of ordinary people and developed his *satyagraha* techniques. Non-violent but highly effective, they led to the Indian Relief Act of 1914 (see page 19). Gandhi the politician soon realized that such methods might be extremely useful elsewhere (*Source 9*).

Gandhi the politician stands outside 10 Downing Street in 1931.

THE STRUGGLE FOR INDEPENDENCE

After the 1919 Amritsar Massacre (see pages 25–26), Gandhi resolved to use *satyagraha* to campaign for India's independence. From 1920, he did so as effective leader of the Indian National Congress, so combining political and other roles (*Source 10*). The high point of *satyagraha* in India was the 1930 Salt March (see page 33), which showed Gandhi's matchless political ability to capture the imagination of India and the world (*Source 11*).

Eventually his 'Quit India' campaign (see page 38), and changes in post-war Britain, led to independence in August 1947.

OTHER CAMPAIGNS

Gandhi did not devote his public life entirely to the struggle with the British. Instead, and especially in the early 1930s, he campaigned for the untouchables and the revival of village India. These were political activities, too, and carried out with the same political skill. Gandhi's *Harijan* walk (see page 36), for example, was a brilliant publicity stunt, while his village programme was designed to produce social and economic changes as great as any that Indian independence might bring.

PERSONAL PROBLEMS

When considering if Gandhi was more politician than saint, it is also important to examine his personal behaviour. Experts have pointed out that, although kind to most people, Gandhi could be harsh to his family. He often lost his temper with his wife and showed little affection to his sons, denying them a proper education and making it hard for them to marry. Harilal (see page 10) suffered most. He died both a drunk and a pauper in 1948.

British prime minister Winston Churchill thought Gandhi a wily politician.

A PRACTICAL POLITICIAN

Gandhi himself denied that he was a saint (*Source 12*), claiming only that he always tried to act in accordance with Truth. His status as a politician, however, is undeniable. Using his unique combination of political skills, he transformed the lives of Indians in both South Africa and the sub-continent, and finally defeated the mighty British Empire (*Source 13*).

SOURCE 10

For he was now truly the 'only one available' for the political job of anchoring the independence movement in the spirit of the Indian masses. And he could now live and function as a whole man; spiritual leader as well as astute lawyer and crafty politician...
(EXTRACT FROM *GANDHI'S TRUTH* BY ERIK H. ERIKSON)

SOURCE 11

...in his superb sense of timing, in his quick intuitive grasp of the balance of forces, in his instinct for effective symbolic action, and in his grasp of the strategy of struggle, Gandhi was one of the most able politicians of his time...
(EXTRACT FROM *GANDHI* BY GEORGE WOODCOCK)

SOURCE 12

To clothe me with sainthood is too early even if it is possible. I myself do not feel a saint in any shape or form.
(EXTRACT FROM *YOUNG INDIA*, 20 JANUARY 1927)

SOURCE 13

Rejecting the epithet [description] of a saint acting as a politician, Gandhi once defined himself as a politician trying to be a saint. If a concern for the collective life of man on this earth is what constitutes a politician... then in every sense Gandhi qualified for the title.
(EXTRACT FROM *GANDHI* BY GEORGE WOODCOCK)

JUDGE
FOR YOURSELF

SATYAGRAHA – CONVERSION OR COERCION?

Gandhi devised the concept of *satyagraha* during his years in South Africa. The term was intended to describe a moral, wholly non-violent type of resistance to injustice that could take various forms. According to Gandhi's ideal, *satyagraha's* main aim was to change opponents' hearts and minds so that they could see the truth of campaigners' arguments, not to make them act differently by exerting force. But did Indians, even Gandhi himself, remain true to this high principle? In other words, was *satyagraha* a means of conversion or coercion? Read both sides of the argument and the sources, then judge for yourself.

CONVERSION?

SOURCE 1

I liked the word [sadagraha, meaning 'firmness in a good cause'], *but it did not fully represent the whole idea I wished it to connote. I therefore corrected it to 'Satyagraha.' Truth* (Satya) *implies love, and firmness* (Agraha) *serves as a synonym for force. I thus began to call the Indian movement 'Satyagraha,' that is the Force which is born of Truth and Love and nonviolence...*
(EXTRACT FROM *SATYAGRAHA IN SOUTH AFRICA* BY M.K. GANDHI)

SOURCE 2

We must try patiently to convert our opponents. If we wish to evolve the spirit of democracy out of slavery, we must be scrupulously exact in our dealings with opponents... We must concede to our opponents the freedom we claim for ourselves and for which we are fighting...
(EXTRACT FROM *YOUNG INDIA* BY M.K. GANDHI, 1922)

A NEW NAME

At a meeting in Johannesburg in 1906, many Indians promised to resist a proposed law designed to discriminate against them (see page 18). Gandhi, who had organized the pledge, wanted any opposition that became necessary to be non-violent.

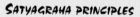
Satyagrahis prevented from continuing a march in 1930 sit down in the road.

However, he did not like the term 'passive resistance', as it suggested weakness, and he wanted to be strong in the power of truth. He therefore asked *Indian Opinion* readers to put forward other ideas and adapted one to produce 'Satyagraha' (*Source 1*).

SATYAGRAHA PRINCIPLES

Gandhi believed *satyagraha* methods should be used to resist oppression only when there was no longer any hope of rational discussion. Their strength was that if talks did break down, they offered an effective means for people to achieve progress without resorting to violence.

Gandhi also tried to ensure *satyagrahas* followed moral guidelines. First, each was to have a clear, justifiable and publicly declared aim; second, protesters were to attempt to convert opponents through non-violence and willing acceptance of punishment (*Source 2*); third, they should be

46

ready to negotiate throughout the protest – the aim was not to defeat or humiliate but to find an outcome acceptable to all. For Gandhi, moral ends had to be achieved by moral means.

SATYAGRAHA IN SOUTH AFRICA

Gandhi organized his first *satyagraha* in 1907 to protest against the Transvaal's Asiatic Registration Act (see page 18). The campaign also became a protest against the tax on indentured labourers. Its high point was in 1913, when Gandhi led a miners' march to Tolstoy Farm (see page 19). Throughout, he remained true to his principles, making clear the march's aim and talking to General Smuts. He also cancelled another *satyagraha* due to take place during a railway strike, believing it would be unfair (*Source 3*). Eventually the *satyagraha* converted the South African authorities and the Indian Relief Act was passed (see page 19).

SATYAGRAHA IN INDIA

Back in India, Gandhi first used *satyagraha* to resolve labour disputes (see page 23). But from 1919, he made non-violent methods part of the independence struggle, declaring this was the best way forward for the country (*Source 4*). There were problems in the early stages – in 1922, Gandhi called off a tax revolt in Bardoli because violence had erupted (see page 27). But later *satyagrahas*, especially the 1930 Salt March and Dharasana Salt Works invasion, all played their part in converting the British. Gandhi's fasts, too, had a great effect (see pages 48–49). By 1947, Britain could resist no longer and granted India its independence.

THE CASE FOR CONVERSION

Gandhi often stated that his aim was to convert the British authorities so that they could first recognize the reality of their oppressive rule in India (*Source 5*), then be persuaded to bring it to an end. Through the skilful and prolonged use of non-violent *satyagraha* techniques, in accordance with strict moral guidelines, he was able to achieve this ambitious goal.

A British policeman seizes two satyagrahis in 1930.

SOURCE 3

It was not part of the tactics of Satyagraha, [Gandhi] explained, to destroy, hurt, humble, or embitter the adversary, or to win a victory by weakening him. Civil resisters hope, by sincerity, chivalry and self-suffering, to convince the opponent's brain and conquer his heart. They never take advantage of the Government's difficulty or form unnatural alliances. (EXTRACT FROM THE LIFE OF MAHATMA GANDHI BY LOUIS FISCHER)

SOURCE 4

Two paths are open before India today, either to introduce the western principle of 'Might is Right,' or to uphold the eastern principle that truth alone conquers, that truth knows no mishap, that the strong and the weak have alike a right to secure justice. (M.K. GANDHI, 1921)

SOURCE 5

My ambition is no less than to convert the British people through non-violence, and thus make them see the wrong they have done to India. I do not seek to harm your people. I want to serve them even as I want to serve my own… (EXTRACT FROM GANDHI'S LETTER TO VICEROY LORD IRWIN, 2 MARCH 1930)

JUDGE
FOR YOURSELF

SATYAGRAHA – CONVERSION OR COERCION?

COERCION?

SOURCE 6

I do not believe in making appeals when there is no force behind them, whether moral or material. Moral force comes from the determination of the appellants [protesters] to do something, to sacrifice something for the sake of making their appeals effective. Even children instinctively know this principle.
(M.K. GANDHI)

SOURCE 7

My fast was not free from a grave defect...I enjoyed very close and cordial relations with the mill-owners and my fast could not but affect their decision. As a satyagrahi I knew that I might not fast against them, but ought to leave them free to be influenced by the millhands' strike alone... With the mill-owners I could only plead; to fast against them would amount to coercion. Yet in spite of my knowledge...I felt I could not help it.
(M.K. GANDHI)

No force?

Gandhi's declared aim was to convert opponents without employing *any* form of force. But in fact, many of his *satyagraha* methods, including his own fasts, were ways of coercing people into doing what he wanted.

Early efforts

Already in South Africa, some of Gandhi's *satyagraha* techniques contained an element of force. Indians' refusal to register had little impact, but the 1913 miners' strike (see page 19) was effective, as it put economic pressure on employers. At the time, even Gandhi accepted *satyagraha* might have to use material as well as moral force (*Source 6*).

Once back in India, Gandhi involved himself in strikes on behalf of workers in Bihar and Ahmedabad (see page 23). Both *satyagrahas* were intended to appeal only to the consciences of unjust employers and to persuade by the power of truth. However, economic pressure was also present, whether Gandhi acknowledged it or not. The Mahatma did accept that the fast he undertook during the Ahmedabad strike had a coercive effect on employers, as they feared for his health (*Source 7*).

Coercive chaos

Satyagrahas in support of Indian home rule also contained coercive features. For example, *hartals* involved withdrawal of labour, and non-cooperation led to the disruption of many institutions. So although Gandhi may have intended the protests to apply only moral pressure, the British responded not with a change of heart, but with practical efforts to end the chaos caused. Likewise,

Textile making is still practised in Ahmedabad.

48

boycotts of British textiles, the 1928 tax revolt and the 1930 salt campaign were seen as an assault on British economic and political interests and dealt with accordingly (*Source 8*).

SATYAGRAHA AND DURAGRAHA

As time passed, the term *satyagraha* was used to cover a growing range of coercive activities. Gandhi even began to describe this method of resistance differently, calling it 'a civilized form of warfare'. In other words, although he still insisted on non-violence, he realized other kinds of force were in use. Gandhi also often suggested that protesters who did not share his principles were involved not in *satyagrahas* but *duragrahas* (*Source 9*), but the difference was often more of intention than effect.

GANDHI'S FASTS

Gandhi's fasts are often classed as a form of *satyagraha*, but some were highly coercive. This was especially true of the 1932 fast in protest against a separate electorate for untouchables (see page 36). By claiming that it was 'to the death', Gandhi was threatening to let himself expire if people did not do as he wished (*Source 10*).

Were Gandhi's fasts a form of coercion?

Under other circumstances, this might have been called moral blackmail.

THE CASE FOR COERCION

The great majority of Gandhi's *satyagraha* protests were not merely truthful appeals to reason and conscience. On the contrary, many included a strong element of economic, political or moral coercion (*Source 11*), and it was this coercion that achieved results.

SOURCE 8

Gandhi...saw the satyagraha *as essentially a moral method. His opponents viewed it very differently. They felt and responded to the impact of political pressure and regarded it basically as a political method like any other, whose moral component was incidental, marginal or even a mere smokescreen.*
(EXTRACT FROM *GANDHI'S POLITICAL PHILOSOPHY* BY BHIKHU PAREKH)

SOURCE 9

To-day I am getting news of satyagraha *being started in many places. Often I wonder whether the so-called* satyagraha *is not really* duragraha [activity based on stubbornness, not truth]. *Whether it is strikes in mills or railways or post offices...it seems as if it is a question of seizing power.*
(EXTRACT FROM GANDHI'S DELHI DIARY, 3 OCTOBER 1947)

SOURCE 10

'there you are. Five years or my life.'
(M.K. GANDHI, RESPONDING TO THE IDEA THAT THE SETTLEMENT TO END THE 1932 FAST SHOULD BE VALID FOR 10 YEARS)

SOURCE 11

[There was] *no real* satyagraha *campaign in India, in the sense that there was no campaign in which moral pressure was the only pressure relied upon.*
(R.C. MAJUMDAR, QUOTED IN *GANDHI'S POLITICAL PHILOSOPHY* BY BHIKHU PAREKH)

JUDGE
FOR YOURSELF

Social Reform – Success or Failure?

Gandhi is best remembered for his major contribution to the Indian independence movement. However, the Mahatma considered that his work to regenerate India from the inside, and in particular to reform its 700,000 villages, was at least equally important. Throughout his life, and especially during the years when he withdrew from politics (see pages 30–31), he devoted much of his time to the 'constructive programme' he had devised to reach these goals. But were Gandhi's attempts to achieve social reform a practical success or an unrealistic failure? Read both sides of the argument and the sources, then judge for yourself.

Success?

SOURCE 1

I would say that if the village perishes India will perish too. India will be no more India. Her own mission in the world will get lost. The revival of the village is possible only when it is no more exploited.
(Extract from a 1936 article by Gandhi in the journal *Harijan*)

SOURCE 2

...an age-old culture is hidden under an encrustment of crudeness. Take away the encrustation, remove his [the Indian peasant's] chronic poverty and illiteracy, and you will find the finest specimen of what a cultured, cultivated free citizen should be.
(Extract from an article by Gandhi in *Harijan*, 1 August 1936)

A moral duty

Gandhi grew up not in a village, but in the city of Porbandar (see page 6). Nevertheless, he knew villages had been at the heart of India's life throughout its long history. Once successful social units, they had fallen into a decline that had, in his view, helped make colonization possible. Under British rule, India's villages had been influenced by Western ideas and suffered economically as a result of Western imports. The Mahatma therefore saw it as his moral duty to revive them (*Source 1*).

Rural rides

Gandhi had spent little time in Indian villages until he returned from South Africa in 1915. But from then on, he made a point of travelling around the country and talking to rural people. What he experienced both depressed and inspired him. He was depressed by the sheer poverty, ignorance and lack of medical care that he found, as well as the evidence of great personal selfishness and dishonesty. However, he was inspired by the huge possibilities for improvement (*Source 2*).

Gandhi encouraged spinning in Indian villages. In 1919, the charka (spinning wheel) became part of the Indian National Congress flag.

50

THE CONSTRUCTIVE PROGRAMME

Gandhi's plans for rural improvement were first put into effect in Bihar, during the indigo-workers' dispute (see page 22). There he set up schools, a medical team and more (*Source 3*). However, it was not until 1920 that he launched his 18-point constructive programme (see page 27) to bring about rural revival, and so to make India worthy of independence.

The constructive programme was very wide-ranging. As well as promoting village industries and particularly the spinning of *khadi* cloth (see page 27), it supported the rights of women and untouchables, and encouraged people to use their native Indian languages rather than English. The programme also included commitments to rural education, health care and improved Hindu-Muslim relations. These diverse aims were all part of one greater goal: the return to *swadeshi*, India's traditional, and in Gandhi's eyes natural, way of life (*Source 4*).

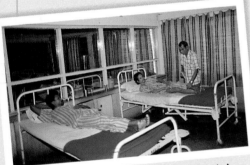

Gandhi's 'constructive workers' did their best to improve village hospitals and health care.

PURSUING THE PROGRAMME

Gandhi pursued his aims tirelessly. Teams of his non-violent and celibate 'constructive workers' set up schools and medical centres, and led *satyagrahas* in support of peasants. Mountains of foreign cloth were burned, bringing ruin to parts of Lancashire (see page 35), but helping revive India's villages. The All-India Village Industries Association (see page 37) also boosted rural economic life. Untouchables benefited, too (see pages 54–57), and all Indians' self-esteem was raised, giving them the courage fully to support Gandhi in his independence campaigns.

A LASTING SUCCESS

Gandhi has been called a 'total revolutionary', who concerned himself as much with social as political reform. He certainly saw his campaign to transform village life in India as an essential part of his mission (*Source 5*), and achieved considerable success. It was a lasting success, too, as after his death many others continued his work (see pages 58–61).

SOURCE 3

He [a doctor Gandhi had appointed] and the volunteers concentrated their energies on making a village ideally clean. They swept the roads and the courtyards, cleaned out the wells, filled up the pools nearby, and lovingly persuaded the villagers to raise volunteers from amongst themselves.
(EXTRACT FROM *AN AUTOBIOGRAPHY* BY M.K. GANDHI)

SOURCE 4

Swadeshi is that spirit in us which restricts us to the use and service of our immediate surroundings to the exclusion of the more remote…Much of the deep poverty of the masses is due to the ruinous departure from Swadeshi in the economic and industrial life. If not an article of commerce had been brought from outside India, she would be today a land flowing with milk and honey.
(EXTRACT FROM *THE WRITINGS OF GANDHI*)

SOURCE 5

For Gandhi, the liberation of India from alien rule was merely the first, if essential first, step towards a radical reconstruction of the social order in India and ultimately in all other countries. As far as India was concerned, this involved…the reconstitution of India as a society of village republics.
(EXTRACT FROM 'THE GANDHIAN MOVEMENT IN INDIA' BY GEOFFREY OSTERGAARD)

SOCIAL REFORM – SUCCESS OR FAILURE?

FAILURE?

SOURCE 6

...our ancestors dissuaded us from luxuries and pleasures. We have managed with the same kind of plough as existed thousands of years ago. We have retained the same kind of cottages that we had in former times and our indigenous [native] education remains the same as before.
(M.K. GANDHI)

SOURCE 7

...only a small minority of India's rural masses has been touched in any important way by the constructive programme which Gandhi devised half a century ago. Many millions of Indian villagers actually live today on a lower level of existence than they endured under the British.
(EXTRACT FROM *GANDHI* BY GEORGE WOODCOCK)

SOURCE 8

How little attention is paid to the convenience of others in streets, in the town as a whole and in trains? We do not hesitate to throw refuse out of our courtyard on to the street; standing in the balcony, we throw out refuse or spit, without pausing to consider whether or not we are inconveniencing the passers-by...
(M.K. GANDHI)

UNREALISTIC PLANS

Without question, Gandhi was committed to radical social reform in India. However, his grand plans were often unrealistic, and by his own admission, many of them ended in disappointment and failure.

VILLAGE VIEW

Gandhi had a romantic view of village life in early India, the kind of life he wished to recreate. He argued that Indian villagers' age-old spiritual understanding meant that they did not need the material goods so important to Westerners (*Source 6*). Building on this rose-tinted image, he set out to create a country of self-sufficient settlements where all were educated, well cared for and content to do only enough work to provide food and other basic needs. Gandhi made some progress towards this goal, but it was minor (*Source 7*). By the 1960s, only 1,500 villages matched his ideals.

TOWN LIFE

Another flaw in Gandhi's social reforms was that they largely ignored cities and towns. The Mahatma was aware of problems in urban areas (*Source 8*), but did not consider cities an essential cornerstone of Indian life in the way villages were. As millions of Indians lived in cities, this was a major oversight, one he really understood only when disturbances broke out there at the time of Partition (see page 41).

(see page 41).

HINDU-MUSLIM TENSIONS

Gandhi regarded the improvement of relations between Hindus and Muslims as a vital part of

In 1922, the ancient Indian settlement of Mohenjo-daro was dug up. This fuelled Gandhi's interest in reviving traditional Indian ways of life.

social reform, and made it a point in his constructive programme (see pages 50–51). However, his sketchy view of Indian history and his unusual openness to all religions made him underestimate the tensions between ordinary members of the two communities. Having trusted that, with goodwill, these tensions would ease, he was sickened by the violence that regularly broke out, especially after independence (see page 41 and *Source 9*).

THE ROLE OF WOMEN

The need for better treatment of women was also outlined in Gandhi's constructive programme. Changes he sought to make included the abolition of child marriage and the provision of better education. But although child marriage is now illegal, it is still practised in places such as Rajasthan. In the same way, although more women are now educated, their literacy rate remains much lower than men's (*Source 10*).

Calcutta in 1935. Gandhi thought little about how to reform India's cities.

A DISAPPOINTING END

After Jawaharlal Nehru formed an independent government in 1947, he soon turned aside from Gandhi's idealistic social reform policies and began to build a nation in the usual mould (see page 60). Unwilling to involve himself in such developments, the Mahatma withdrew completely from politics and advised his constructive workers to do likewise (*Source 11*).

AN OBVIOUS FAILURE

Gandhi's dreams of social reform were largely unfulfilled by the time of his death in 1948. Despite more than 30 years of intense effort by both the great man and his supporters, his plans were an obvious failure.

SOURCE 9

Anger breeds revenge and the spirit of revenge is to-day responsible for all the horrible happenings here and elsewhere. What good will it do the Muslims to avenge the happenings in Delhi or for the Sikhs and Hindus to avenge cruelties on our co-religionists in the Frontier and West Punjab?… I implore you all to stop your insane actions at once. Let not future generations say that we lost the sweet bread of freedom because we could not digest it. Remember that unless we stop this madness the name of India will be mud in the eyes of the world.
(EXTRACT FROM GANDHI'S DIARY ENTRY FOR 12 SEPTEMBER 1947)

SOURCE 10

INDIAN LITERACY RATE % (1996)

Men	62
Women	34

SOURCE 11

Politics have today become corrupt. Anybody who goes into them is contaminated. Let us keep out of them altogether. Our influence will grow thereby.
(M.K. GANDHI)

AID TO THE UNTOUCHABLES – SUCCESS OR FAILURE?

From childhood onwards, Gandhi detested the mistreatment of India's approximately 50 million untouchables, that is non-caste Hindus (see page 28). Once he was an adult and a respected leader, therefore, he did all he could to help them, and even gave them a new name – *Harijan*. But did Gandhi treat untouchables with the respect he claimed that they deserved? And did his efforts really have any lasting effect? In other words was Gandhi's aid to the untouchables a success or a failure? Read both sides of the argument and the sources, then judge for yourself.

SUCCESS?

SOURCE 1

I regard untouchability as the greatest blot on Hinduism....I was hardly yet 12 when this idea had dawned on me. A scavenger named Uka, an untouchable, used to attend our house for cleaning latrines...If I accidentally touched Uka, I was asked to perform the ablutions [ritual washing], and though I naturally obeyed, it was not without smilingly protesting that untouchability was not sanctioned by religion...
(EXTRACT FROM *YOUNG INDIA*)

SOURCE 2

Though in South Africa my untouchable friends used to come to my place and live and feed with me, my wife and other women did not seem quite to relish the admission into the Ashram of the untouchable friends. My eyes and ears easily detected their indifference, if not their dislike...
(EXTRACT FROM *AN AUTOBIOGRAPHY* BY M.K. GANDHI)

THE FIRST UNTOUCHABLES

The concept of untouchability developed about 3,000 years ago, when Aryans from northern India (see page 28) invaded the South. The newcomers divided the existing inhabitants into the castes to which they themselves belonged. But the people who had fled from their advance were not granted caste status, and when they returned to live around the edges of new settlements were often given dirty jobs to do, such as taking away rubbish. In this way, they became the first untouchables.

EARLY EXPERIENCES

By Gandhi's time, there were strict rules governing the treatment of untouchables, the most important of which was that caste Hindus were not allowed to touch them. Even as a boy, Gandhi found this ridiculous, but still performed the rituals that were necessary to cleanse himself if

Gandhi during his 1933 to 1934 tour for Harijan 'upliftment'.

contact occurred (*Source 1*). Although he tried not to touch them, he could not avoid seeing untouchables around him every day. Most were employed to clean latrines or streets, jobs that caste Hindus would not do.

JUDGE
FOR YOURSELF

UNTOUCHABILITY IN THE ASHRAM

Gandhi made the first move in his campaign for the untouchables by accepting them in his Satyagraha ashram (see page 22). This caused uproar among many members of the community, including his wife, Kasturbai (*Source 2*). However, he persisted, even to the extent of adopting a young untouchable girl called Lakshmi. He also made it clear that everyone was expected to do their share of the menial tasks.

THE EPIC FAST

In 1920, Gandhi made removal of untouchability one of the points in his constructive programme (see page 27). But the next major milestone in his journey on behalf of the untouchables did not come until 1932. In that year, Britain suggested the introduction of a separate electorate for them (see page 36), an idea Gandhi found unacceptable. He therefore published a statement explaining he would fast until a better agreement had been reached (*Source 3*), then on 20 September stopped eating. A solution was found within six days and many caste Hindus began warily to change their behaviour towards untouchables.

THE HARIJAN PILGRIMAGE

In 1933, Gandhi set up the Harijan Sevak Sangh, an organization to help untouchables, and the *Harijan* journal for the same purpose. Later that year, he began a 10-month tour of India to raise awareness and collect funds (see page 36). In this way, he brought the untouchable cause to public attention and started to convert hearts and minds (*Source 4*). It was largely thanks to his persistence that untouchability was abolished in 1947 and the *Harijan* became a scheduled caste with full rights.

A 1942 copy of Harijan, the first in a new series.

A GREAT SUCCESS

Gandhi expressed his condemnation of untouchability (*Source 5*) and genuinely felt the untouchables' plight (*Source 6*). His championing of their cause made it the subject of public debate and produced real improvements. His aid to the untouchables was a success.

SOURCE 3

No patched-up agreement between Caste Hindus and rival Depressed Classes (untouchables) will answer the purpose. The agreement to be valid has to be real. If the Hindu mass mind is not yet prepared to banish untouchability root and branch [completely] it must sacrifice me without the slightest hesitation.
(M.K. GANDHI)

SOURCE 4

'Touchables' had to be taught 'patiently' by practice and example that untouchability is a sin against humanity and to be atoned for, and the untouchables that they should cease to fear the touchables and not show untouchability amongst themselves.'
(EXTRACT FROM *THE LAST PHASE* BY PYARELAL, QUOTING GANDHI)

SOURCE 5

...I have never been able to reconcile myself to untouchability. I have always regarded it as an excrescence [unwanted growth]. It is true that it has been handed down to us from generations, but so are many evil practices even to this day.
(EXTRACT FROM *YOUNG INDIA*)

SOURCE 6

I do not want to be re-born, but if I have to be re-born I should be re-born an untouchable so that I may share their sorrows...
(M.K. GANDHI)

Aid to the Untouchables — Success or Failure?

Failure?

Source 7

Gandhi saw it [untouchability] as *a blot on the Hindu landscape and made it the sole responsibility of the high-caste Hindus to fight against it. The untouchables themselves, reduced to passive and pathetic symbols of high-caste Hindu tyranny, were not involved in the struggle for their emancipation, a strange attitude in a man who everywhere else wanted the victims to fight for themselves.*
(Extract from *Gandhi's Political Philosophy* by Bhikhu Parekh)

Source 8

The [Harijan Sevak Sangh's] function being to discharge a debt rather than confer a privilege, its executive was manned exclusively by those who had to do the atonement.
'*How can caste Hindus look after the interests of the Harijans? How can they realise the feelings of the classes who have suffered so long at their hands?' Gandhiji was finally asked.*
(Extract from *The Last Phase* by Pyarelal)

Confused motives
Gandhi did both condemn and fight against untouchability. Nevertheless, his motives and methods were sometimes confused, and the results of his efforts were disappointing – untouchability still exists in practice today.

From high to low
Critics of Gandhi's dealings with the untouchables point out one major difficulty of his approach. Instead of encouraging and enabling the *Harijan* to fight for themselves, he treated them as unfortunate victims that caste Hindus had to rescue (*Source 7*). In particular, he did not allow them to fill high-ranking positions in the Harijan Sevak Sangh (see pages 54–55), a fact that outcastes themselves criticized (*Source 8*).

Nehru did not always agree with Gandhi's ideas.

The epic fast
Gandhi portrayed his epic 1932 fast against a separate untouchable electorate (see page 36) as a personal sacrifice for the untouchables' benefit. Some experts question this view, pointing out that many untouchables actually wanted their own electorate. Knowing this, and despite the fact that the British had made important concessions, Gandhi stubbornly went ahead with his fast. Jawaharlal Nehru (see page 32) and others roundly criticized him for it (*Source 9*).
Among Gandhi's untouchable opponents on this issue was the leading activist Dr Bhimrao Ramji Ambedkar, a US-trained lawyer who had represented his people at the 1931 Round Table Conference (see page 34–35). His stance had its own morality, yet Gandhi was either unable or unwilling to see it, showing again that he

found it difficult to let untouchables take control of their own destiny (*Source 10*).

THE END OF UNTOUCHABILITY?

The work of Gandhi and his supporters certainly played a large part in the official abolition of untouchability at the time of independence. Yet legal change is not necessarily the same as real change. Although the most obvious forms of discrimination have disappeared in many places – untouchables never now have to stand at fixed distances from caste Hindus, for example – more subtle prejudice persists. In particular, caste Hindus still rarely socialize with former untouchables and may quietly prevent them from winning promotion at work or important public positions. In remote villages, the situation can be far worse.

The caste system as a whole still pervades Indian society. Gandhi did not condemn the system outright (*Source 11*), but considered that it had become seriously corrupted over time. Today caste makes it very difficult for people to change their role in society, and helps to trap the poor, who make up 60 per cent of India's people, in their poverty. Many people at all levels work abroad in order to escape this rigidity.

In India's modern cities, the caste system is weakening. But in villages, it is still strong.

A PARTIAL FAILURE

Gandhi's work on behalf of the untouchables, though always well-meaning, was deeply flawed, as it denied them their own voice. In addition, though his efforts did produce great benefits, they by no means wiped out the caste distinctions that still blight India today.

SOURCE 9

I felt angry with him at his religious and sentimental approach to a political question, and his frequent references to God in connection with it.
(EXTRACT FROM THE AUTOBIOGRAPHY OF JAWAHARLAL NEHRU AS QUOTED IN *THE LIFE OF MAHATMA GANDHI* BY LOUIS FISCHER)

SOURCE 10

Gandhi's lack of respect for Ambedkar's position was unfortunate, not only because he failed to honor the Untouchable leader as a person, but also because he failed to recognize the morality of Ambedkar's mission… By insisting on the right of distinct representation for his people Ambedkar's aim was to bring them, through those means, into the mainstream of Indian life.
(EXTRACT FROM 'SHORING UP THE SAINT' BY MARK JUERGENSMEYER)

SOURCE 11

Gandhi thought that the much-maligned caste system…was, in its original and 'pure' form, a result of years of research into the nature of man and society and designed to create a social order based on the ineliminable differences [differences that cannot be eliminated] in the human temperament and level of moral and spiritual evolution.
(EXTRACT FROM *GANDHI'S POLITICAL PHILOSOPHY* BY BHIKHU PAREKH)

GANDHI'S IDEALS – LASTING OR LOST?

In the years since Gandhi's death in 1948, people right across the world, and especially Martin Luther King, Jr. in the USA (see below), have claimed to base their protest movements on Gandhi's ideals of non-violence, truth and moral regeneration. But were his policies really transferrable, or were they too closely linked to the Mahatma, his time and his country, to be of use elsewhere? In other words, have Gandhi's ideals and methods been lasting or are they now lost? Read both sides of the argument and the sources, then judge for yourself.

LASTING?

SOURCE 1

The Gita *is prepared to go to the lowest, the weakest and least cultured of men. And it goes to him, not to keep him where he is, but to grasp him by the hand and lift him up.*
(VINOBA BHAVE)

SOURCE 2

Vinoba Bhave, a constructive worker...was offered by a local landlord 100 acres of land as a gift for distribution to the landless laborers in the village. Vinoba saw the gift as a sign from God, indicating the way in which non-violent change could and should be pursued. Thus was born the campaign for Bhoodan – the voluntary gift of land to the landless.
(EXTRACT FROM 'THE GANDHIAN MOVEMENT IN INDIA SINCE THE DEATH OF GANDHI' BY GEOFFREY OSTERGAARD)

ENDURING IDEALS
Gandhi's ideals and methods have endured both in his Indian homeland and elsewhere. By turning to them, protesters have been able to pursue their aims without violence as he tried to do.

THE INDIAN EXPERIENCE
In India, Gandhi was able to pass on his ideals to the 'constructive workers' in person (see page 27). Shortly after his death, in March 1948, they set up an organization called Sarva Seva Sangh (Association for the Service of All) that aimed to ensure his social reforms were continued. It quickly produced a plan to bring about *sarvodaya*, the general welfare of all, and opposed much government thinking.

A related, more dramatic legacy was the work of Vinoba Bhave, who like Gandhi was inspired by the *Bhagavad Gita* (*Source 1*). In 1951 Bhave began a pilgrimage around India to encourage donations of land to the landless. By 1958, he had distributed some 2 million hectares to about 500,000 people. In so doing, like Gandhi before him, he helped to revive India's villages and support its poorest inhabitants (*Source 2*).

Vinoba Bhave addresses a meeting in the Indian city of Agra in 1960.

JUDGE
FOR YOURSELF

GANDHI AND KING

Martin Luther King, Jr. the American preacher and activist for black civil rights, openly acknowledged his debt to the ideals and methods developed by Gandhi (*Source 3*). King was born in 1929 in the American South, where segregation and prejudice were the daily experiences of black people. As a young man, he yearned to help his community, but as a Christian was reluctant to turn to violence. At the same time, he felt that non-violent protest was weak and achieved little.

King discovered Gandhi's works in his 20s, when he was studying at Crozer Seminary in Pennsylvania. They offered him a third way between unacceptable violence and ineffective non-violence: *satyagraha*, non-violence based on the power of truth (*Source 4*). From the mid-1950s, King organized many non-violent marches and other protests. They finally led Congress to pass two historic laws: the Civil Rights Act (1964) and the Voting Rights Act (1965). As a result, segregation was outlawed and black people won the unequivocal right to vote.

ACROSS THE WORLD

Thousands of other people have used and developed Gandhi's non-violent techniques since his death. In the early 1970s, for example, American protesters campaigned non-violently for their country's withdrawal from the Vietnam War. US troops were pulled out in 1973. In Britain in 1981, a group of women set up camp at Greenham Common airbase to protest against the siting of American cruise missiles there. In Japan, a non-violent *sarvodaya* movement (see page 58) has been founded, and in Costa Rica there is even a UN University for Peace.

A LASTING LEGACY

Gandhi's ideals were timeless and his skilful application of them to solve political and economic problems provided the world with a shining example of how to protest without violence. His legacy will not fade.

SOURCE 3

If humanity is to progress, Gandhi is inescapable. He lived, thought, and acted, inspired by the vision of humanity evolving toward a world of peace and harmony. We may ignore him at our own risk.
(MARTIN LUTHER KING)

SOURCE 4

I can't make myself believe that God wants me to hate. I'm tired of violence. And I'm not going to let my oppressor dictate to me what method I must use. We have a power, power that can't be found in Molotov cocktails, but we do have a power. Power that cannot be found in bullets and guns, but we have a power. It is a power as old as the insights of Jesus of Nazareth and as modern as the techniques of Mahatma Gandhi.
(MARTIN LUTHER KING)

A 1960s' demonstration against the Vietnam War in Washington, D.C., the US capital.

GANDHI'S IDEALS — LASTING OR LOST?

LOST?

SOURCE 5

A COMPARISON OF GOALS AND PROGRAMS ADVOCATED BY GANDHI AND KING

Gandhi

–Self-purification as a condition for achieving political independence (e.g. fasts)

–Development of village industries and sanitation

–Adult education and health programs

–Elimination of liquor [alcohol]

–Use of a spinning wheel in every home

–Organization of Labor satyagrahas (e.g. Ahmedabad in 1918)

King

–Federal grants for housing, employment, and education

–1963 Bill of rights for the disadvantaged

–Government-guaranteed income

–Development of Black co-ops

–Breadbasket program [helping black people in Chicago find work]

–Organization of unions

(CHART TAKEN FROM 'THE INFLUENCE OF GANDHI ON MARTIN LUTHER KING, JR.' BY THOMAS KILGORE, JR.)

UNIQUE SKILLS

Gandhi was an extraordinary human being who combined a deep spirituality with matchless political skills. He was also precisely the right man for India at precisely the right moment. Since his death in 1948, many have tried to follow in his footsteps, but no one has succeeded.

INDIAN DEVELOPMENTS

Shortly before his assassination, Gandhi suggested the Indian National Congress replace itself with a Lok Sevak Sangh (Association for the Service of the People). This body would devote itself not to political power but to social reform. It was not to be. Nehru had already begun to rebuild India as an ordinary state, and once Gandhi was dead there was no one of equal stature to argue for non-violence and regeneration.

The *sarvodaya* movement (see pages 58–59) shared many of Gandhi's principles, and in the 1970s under Jayaprakash Narayan's leadership, protested effectively against the authoritarian government of Indira Gandhi. However, it has never been able to offer an enduring and credible alternative to the party politics that now holds sway.

Prime minister of India from 1966 to 1977 and 1980 to 1984, Indira Gandhi was not related to Mahatma Gandhi.

GANDHI AND KING

Martin Luther King, Jr. (see pages 58–59) is the man many believe has come closest to following Gandhi's example. Yet there were major differences between the two leaders.

Although no fundamentalist, King was a committed Christian, while Gandhi was a Hindu with very fluid religious views. King did not share Gandhi's need to give up sex, good food and other pleasures for the sake of his cause. Importantly, King never lost faith in government, while Gandhi grew disillusioned with political power, so their goals were different (*Source 5*).

King used Gandhi's non-violent tactics to great effect in the rural South of America, but when he tried to help black people in northern cities such as Chicago during the mid-1960s, he had far less success. Some experts consider that this was because Gandhi's techniques were developed mainly in and for rural India, so did not work elsewhere.

AROUND THE WORLD

Gandhi's ideals and methods have been adopted across the world (*Source 6*). In addition to the examples given on pages 58–59, non-violent protesters have included environmental groups such as Greenpeace. However violent protest, planned or unintentional, remains common. For example, some 21st-century campaigners against the globalization of trade have used violence at demonstrations in Seattle London and Genoa, and some animal rights activists also adopt violent techniques.

GAIN AND LOSS

Gandhi's achievements showed the world the possibilities of non-violent protest, and it has since been widely used. But few participants have been able to match Gandhi's rigorous morality and selflessness. King, whom many see as Gandhi's moral equal, was nevertheless a different man with a different cause. So in the sense that no one could bring Gandhi's own ideals to life in his own way, they are lost.

SOURCE 6

...we have seen a remarkable geographical and theoretical expansion of nonviolent political action since the death of Gandhi 40 years ago. It has spread to every part of the world, is known to and used by larger numbers of people of every social class, and constantly develops new forms of expression. The vitality of the concept is so striking that it may prove to be the most revolutionary idea of the twentieth century.
(EXTRACT FROM 'GANDHI'S RELEVANCE TODAY' BY JAMES W. GOULD. THE ARTICLE WAS WRITTEN IN THE LATE 1980s)

Anti-globalization demonstrators at the 1999 World Trade Organization meeting in Seattle, USA. Many were peaceful, but violence still erupted.

GLOSSARY

ahimsa Non-violence

anaemia A disorder caused by having insufficient red cells in the blood. Anaemia sufferers are weak and find it hard to breathe.

Anglo-Indian An English person who has lived in India for many years and often adopted some elements of Indian life. (The term can also mean a person of mixed English and Indian ancestry.)

ashram A Hindu religious community, especially one where a holy man lives.

avatar A human or other form taken by a Hindu god on Earth.

Ayurvedic (Of medicines) based on an ancient Hindu book about medicines and healing techniques called the Ayurveda. 'Ayurveda' literally means 'life knowledge'.

Bhagavad Gita A Hindu holy book written in the form of a poem in the Sanskrit language about 2,300 years ago. The book's name means 'Song of the Blessed'.

Boer A descendant of the Dutch or Huguenot (French Protestant) people who settled in South Africa from the 17th century. 'Boer' is Dutch for 'farmer'.

British Empire Britain and the territories that it conquered and colonized from the 17th century onwards. The Empire reached its greatest extent in 1918, when it included about a quarter of the world's population and area. India was the first British colony to gain its independence, in 1947. It was soon followed by many more, and the Empire gradually disintegrated.

Buddhism A religion that began in India in about 500 BC. It grew from Hinduism and is based on the teaching of a prince called Gautama Siddhartha, who was given the title ' Buddha' ('enlightened one'). Buddhism flourished in India for well over 1,000 years, but from the 8th century AD most Indian Buddhists became Hindus again.

caste Any of the four main hereditary classes into which Hindus are traditionally divided. These are Brahmans (priests), Kshatriyas (warriors), Vaisyas (merchants) and Sudras (farmers and peasants). Gandhi was born into the Vaisya caste.

celibate Not engaging in or involving sexual activity.

colonial Of or relating to a colony (see below).

colony A territory governed by the rulers of another state.

concentration camp A camp where large numbers of people are imprisoned.

Congress The law-making body of the US government. It consists of two houses, the Senate and the House of Representatives.

deportation Forced removal from a country; expulsion.

dominion A self-governing nation that still remained part of the British Empire.

East India Company A trading company set up by Queen Elizabeth I in 1600. Its first aim was to pursue British trade with the East Indies, but the Dutch forced it out of the region. The Company therefore concentrated on trade with India, much of which it administered for many years. Following the Indian Mutiny of 1857-1858, however, the British government took over. The Company was dissolved in 1874.

First World War A major war that lasted from 1914 to 1918 and that involved many countries. Britain and its Empire fought alongside France, Russia (until 1917) and the USA (from 1917) to defeat Germany, Austria-Hungary and their allies.

franchise The right to vote in elections.

fundamentalist A person who follows their religion very strictly, usually believing that every word of their holy book (e.g. the Bible or the Qur'an) is literally true.

Gujarati The official language of the Indian state of Gujarat, and Gandhi's native tongue. It belongs to the same group of languages as Hindi, the official language of India.

guru A Sikh or Hindu religious teacher and spiritual guide.

Harijan *see* **untouchable**.

hartal A general strike, that is a strike undertaken by workers from all or most industries and professions, not just one.

hill station A town or other settlement in northern India that is on high ground and so cooler than surrounding, lower regions.

Hindi The official language of India, which is spoken by about a third of the country's population.

indigo A tropical plant that is used to make a blue dye. Now the dye can also be made in laboratories.

indentured labourer A labourer who has signed a contract agreeing to work overseas for a fixed time in return for travel expenses, food and lodging. Britain employed many indentured labourers from India on farms and plantations in other British colonies. These workers were often treated little better than slaves.